RESISTANCE AS IDEA
AND ACTION

Resistance As Idea And Action

THE EPIC STRUGGLE AGAINST OPPRESSION AND TYRANNY THROUGHOUT HISTORY

GEW Reports and Analyses Team

Hichem Karoui

Global East-West (London)

Copyright © 2024 by GEW Reports and Analyses Team
Collection: Resistances. Under the Supervision of Dr Hichem Karoui.
Global East-West For Studies and Publishing

All rights reserved. No part of this book may be reproduced in any manner whatsoever without written permission except in the case of brief quotations embodied in critical articles and reviews.

First Printing, 2024

Contents

Copyright	iv

Preface		**1**
1	Introduction	8
2	Ancient Civilisations and the Birth of Resistance	17
3	The Middle Ages: Religion and Resistance	22
4	The Enlightenment Era: Resistance as Intellectual Rebellion	27
5	XIXth Century: The Age of Revolutions and Nationalism	33
6	Colonial Resistances: The Struggle for Identity and Autonomy	37
7	The World Wars: Resistance Against Occupiers and Tyrants	43
8	The Cold War and Beyond: Ideological Resistances	51

9	Modern Era: Digital Revolutions and The Power of Information	60
10	Resistance in Arts and Culture	65
11	The Philosophy of Resistance in the 21st Century	72
12	Resistance in Literature	78
13	Conclusion	85
14	Post-Scriptum: A Historical Account of Palestinian Resistance to Zionist Colonialism and Oppression, From 1947 to 2024.	91
References For Further Reading		147

Preface

The Epic Struggle Against Oppression and Tyranny Throughout History

In every era, from the early days of human civilisation until the present time, people have consistently fought against oppression and tyranny. This arduous struggle for freedom and justice has shaped societies, propelled revolutions, and fostered a collective conscience against the subjugation of human rights and dignity. From ancient times to the transformative movements of the 21st century, the unwavering resistance of individuals and communities against oppressive forces has left an indelible mark on the course of history.

1. Introduction

The fight against oppression and tyranny is deeply ingrained in the human spirit. Individuals and communities have time and again risen against forces that sought to suppress their freedoms, silence their voices, and deny them their basic human rights. Over the centuries, countless people have made immense sacrifices, challenging the status quo and paving the way for a fairer and more just society. This article traces the epic struggle against oppression and tyranny, exploring pivotal moments, movements, and individuals that have shaped the world we inhabit today.

2. Definition of Oppression and Tyranny

Before delving into historical accounts, it is crucial to define the terms "oppression" and "tyranny." Oppression refers to the unjust exercise of power, often involving the systematic persecution, marginalisation, or suppression of specific groups or individuals. Tyranny, on the other hand, implies the arbitrary and cruel exercise of power by a single ruler or an authoritarian regime. Both oppression and tyranny have been challenges faced by humanity throughout history, giving rise to powerful resistance movements.

3. Early Resistance Movements

3.1 Ancient Civilisations

Even in ancient times, people resisted oppression and tyranny. From the Hebrews' journey to escape Egyptian slavery to the rebellions against tyrannical rulers in Mesopotamia and Persia, the struggle against domination was an inherent part of human existence. Ancient civilisations witnessed the defiance of oppressed populations and their pursuit of freedom, providing early examples of resistance against oppressive regimes.

3.2 The Fight for Freedom in Medieval Times

The medieval period saw numerous uprisings against feudal lords and monarchs. Peasant rebellions like the Jacquerie in France and the German Peasants' War demonstrated the determination of the lower classes to challenge the oppressive feudal system. Additionally, the Magna Carta signed in 1215 in England marked a crucial step towards curbing the absolute power of the monarchy, ensuring basic rights and liberties for the English people.

4. Enlightenment and Revolutionary Movements

4.1 The Age of Enlightenment

The Age of Enlightenment, spanning the 17th and 18th centuries, brought about a profound shift in human thought. Intellectuals and philosophers advocated for reason, individual liberty, and the pursuit of happiness. The ideas of thinkers like John Locke, Montesquieu, and Voltaire challenged the oppressive rule of absolutist monarchies, inspiring future revolutions.

4.2 American Revolution

The American Revolution, a pivotal moment in the struggle against tyranny, saw the American colonies rising against British colonial rule. Driven by principles of liberty and self-governance, the revolutionaries fought for independence and established the United States of America, becoming an enduring symbol of freedom and democracy.

4.3 French Revolution

The French Revolution, influenced by Enlightenment ideas, witnessed a dramatic overthrow of the monarchy and the establishment of the First French Republic. The revolutionaries sought to dismantle the oppressive social and political structures, championing principles of liberty, equality, and fraternity, albeit amidst tumultuous times.

5. Struggles for Independence and Decolonisation

5.1 Indian Independence Movement

The Indian independence movement led by Mahatma Gandhi stands as one of the most remarkable struggles against colonial oppression. Through nonviolent civil disobedience, Gandhi and millions of Indians fought against British rule, ultimately gaining independence in 1947. This movement became a model for other oppressed nations, inspiring similar struggles for liberation.

5.2 African Independence Movements

Across Africa, the mid-20th century witnessed a wave of movements and revolutions aimed at ending colonial rule. Led by figures such as Nelson Mandela in South Africa, Kwame Nkrumah in Ghana, and Jomo Kenyatta in Kenya, these movements pushed for self-determination and the elimination of colonisation from the continent.

6. Modern Civil Rights Movements

6.1 African-American Civil Rights Movement

The African-American Civil Rights Movement in the United States was a transformative struggle against racial oppression and discrimination. Led by remarkable figures like Martin Luther King Jr., Rosa Parks, and Malcolm X, this movement sought to end segregation, secure voting rights, and achieve equal treatment under the law. Through nonviolent protests, boycotts, and legal challenges, the movement gained significant victories and paved the way for greater equality.

6.2 Women's Rights Movement

The fight for women's rights has been a longstanding battle against the patriarchal systems that have hindered women's empowerment and progress. From the suffragette movement demanding the right to vote to contemporary campaigns for gender equality, women have consistently challenged societal norms and fought for equal rights, reproductive rights, and an end to gender-based discrimination.

7. Contemporary Struggles for Freedom and Democracy

7.1 Arab Spring

The Arab Spring, which began in 2010 across various countries in the Middle East and North Africa, marked a turning point in the struggle for freedom and democracy in the region. Protests erupted against authoritarian regimes, demanding political reforms, economic justice, and respect for human rights. Though the outcomes varied across countries, the Arab Spring remains a symbol of people's aspiration for self-determination and democratic governance.

7.2 Palestinian Struggle Against Israeli Occupation

The Palestinian struggle against Israeli occupation and tyranny is a crucial and ongoing chapter in the fight against oppression. The Palestinian people have long endured the consequences of the Israeli-Palestinian conflict, which has resulted in displacement, loss of land, and restricted freedoms. Palestinians have organised resistance movements to assert their right to self-determination and to seek justice and equality.

The Palestinian Liberation Organisation (PLO) was established in 1964 as a representative body for the Palestinian people, dedicated to resisting the Israeli occupation and advocating for their rights. The PLO played a significant role in mobilising support for the Palestinian cause on an international level and in fostering unity among Palestinians.

Over the years, multiple uprisings, known as intifadas, have erupted as a response to Israeli policies and actions. The First Intifada, which began in 1987, saw widespread civil disobedience and acts of resistance by Palestinians, demanding an end to the Israeli occupation and the establishment of a Palestinian state. The Second Intifada, starting in 2000, was marked by increased violence and armed confrontations.

Despite the challenges and complexities of the Israeli-Palestinian conflict, there have been ongoing efforts to find a just and lasting solution. Numerous peace negotiations, such as the Oslo Accords in the 1990s, aimed to establish a framework for peaceful coexistence between Israelis and Palestinians. However, the path to peace remains elusive, as issues such as borders, settlements, and the status of Jerusalem continue to be contentious points of disagreement.

The Palestinian struggle continues to garner international attention and support. Advocacy groups, civil society organisations, and activists worldwide stand in solidarity with the Palestinian people and call for an end to the occupation, the recognition of their rights, and the establishment of an independent, viable Palestinian state.

It is important to note that perspectives on the Israeli-Palestinian conflict differ significantly, and there are varying narratives surrounding the struggle. The history of the conflict is marked by complex political, historical, and religious dynamics, making it a deeply nuanced issue that requires comprehensive and inclusive dialogue.

7.3 Black Lives Matter Movement

The Black Lives Matter (BLM) movement emerged as a powerful response to systemic racism, police brutality, and social injustice faced by Black communities, particularly in the United States. Through protests, awareness campaigns, and advocacy, BLM aims to dismantle structural racism, demanding accountability and equal treatment for all individuals, regardless of their race or ethnicity.

8. *Conclusion*

The epic struggle against oppression and tyranny has transcended time and borders, uniting individuals and communities in their quest for justice and freedom. From ancient civilisations to modern movements, humanity has consistently risen against oppressive systems, challenging unjust power structures and advocating for equality, dignity, and human rights. While the road to liberation is often rugged and fraught with sacrifice, the indomitable spirit of those who resist tyranny continues to shape a more equitable and inclusive world.

1

Introduction

Welcome to the world of resistance, where individuals and communities rise against injustice, oppression, and tyranny. Throughout history, resistance has played a vital and transformative role in shaping societies, challenging the status quo, and advocating for change. From ancient civilisations to the modern era, acts of resistance have sparked revolutions, inspired social movements, and forever changed the course of human history.

The Seeds of Resistance in Ancient Civilisations:

Our exploration begins in the early days of humanity, where the seeds of resistance were sown in the fertile ground of ancient civilisations. In ancient Egypt, the construction of monumental structures such as the Great Pyramids often relied on a labour force of peasants and workers who, at times, staged strikes or walkouts to express their discontent and demand better working conditions. These demonstrations of solidarity and collective action exemplify the power of unity in resisting oppressive regimes.

Moving further in time, we encounter the ancient Greek city-states, renowned for their contributions to the foundations of modern democracy. Here, resistance took on a philosophical dimension. Figures such as Socrates, who challenged conventional beliefs and questioned the authority of the Athenian state, faced persecution and ultimately chose death over capitulation. Their intellectual resistance, rooted in the pursuit of truth, reason, and individual autonomy, inspired generations to question and challenge prevailing norms and societal structures.

Feudalism and Peasant Uprisings:

Transitioning to the medieval period, we find ourselves in an era dominated by feudalism – an economic and social system marked by a stark division of power and wealth. In this system, peasants toiled under the dominion of feudal lords, enduring heavy burdens and oppressive conditions.

However, resistance was not extinguished. Peasant uprisings, such as the Jacquerie in 14th century France and the German Peasants' War in the 16th century, exemplified the determination of the oppressed classes to challenge the feudal order and dismantle the system that perpetuated their suffering. These movements were characterised by demands for fair treatment, abolishing serfdom, and a more equitable distribution of land and resources.

The Enlightenment and the Intellectual Rebellion:

As Europe transitioned from the feudal age to the Enlightenment, resistance took on new forms and found its voice in intellectual rebellion. The Enlightenment created a philosophical movement that challenged traditional authority and extolled the virtues of reason, knowledge, and individual rights. Prominent thinkers such as John Locke, Voltaire, and Jean-Jacques Rousseau disseminated ideas that questioned the legitimacy of absolutist monarchies and advocated for establishing more representative and accountable forms of governance. Their writings served as a call to arms for resistance against oppressive regimes, paving the way for democratic revolutions in the late 18th and early 19th centuries.

Age of Revolutions and Nationalism:

The dawn of the 19th century marked a period of radical change as waves of nationalism surged across Europe and the Americas. Resistance movements took centre stage as people sought to reclaim their cultural identities and assert their desires for self-governance. The American Revolution, fuelled by a commitment to the principles of liberty and self-determination, severed ties with British colonial rule and established a new democratic republic. Similarly, the French Revolution, ignited by equality, fraternity, and liberty ideals, saw the French people overthrow the monarchy and set in motion a new era of extraordinary political and social changes.

In addition to these seminal events, numerous uprisings unfolded across Europe during this era, driven by a potent blend of nationalist fervour, economic grievances, and demands for social justice. The Hungarian Revolution of 1848, the Greek War of Independence, and the various uprisings against oppressive colonial rule in Latin America demonstrate the immense power of collective resistance in dismantling oppressive systems and ushering in new eras of independence and social progress.

Colonial Resistance and Struggles for Independence:

The colonial era witnessed resistance taking on a new dimension as indigenous populations, subjected to centuries of colonial rule, began to challenge the oppressive yoke of foreign powers. The struggle for independence became a battle for sovereignty, cultural preservation, and the rejection of the dehumanising effects of colonisation. The Haitian Revolution (1791-1804) stands as a remarkable testament to resistance. Born out of the enduring spirit of freedom and the desire for emancipation, enslaved Africans and their allies rose against the powerful French empire, successfully establishing the first nation in the Western Hemisphere led by former slaves.

Similar resistance movements birthed national independence across Latin America, as revolutionary leaders such as Simón Bolívar and José de San Martín led campaigns against colonial powers, toppling oppressive regimes and forging new nations. In Asia, the Indian subcontinent witnessed the valiant resistance of figures like Mahatma Gandhi, who advocated for nonviolent means of resistance against British colonial rule. Through civil disobedience, boycotts, and nonviolent protests, they challenged the moral authority of the oppressor and secured independence for their respective nations.

World Wars and Occupations:

The early 20th century brought unprecedented challenges as the world was consumed by two devastating world wars and the occupation of entire nations. In this backdrop, resistance took on diverse and resilient forms. Occupied countries experienced the emergence of underground networks and partisan warfare as resistance fighters courageously engaged in sabotage, espionage, and acts of sabotage against occupying forces. These clandestine efforts served to preserve national identity and disrupt the oppressor's grip.

The bravery of individuals and communities during this period is exemplified by the French Resistance, who defiantly resisted Nazi occupation through clandestine activities and acts of sabotage. The Warsaw Uprising, a valiant but ill-fated rebellion by the Polish Home Army against Nazi forces, stands as a testament to the indomitable spirit of those who refused to surrender their dignity and freedom.

Beyond Ideological Divides:

In the aftermath of World War II, the world became polarised by competing political ideologies during the Cold War. Resistance movements operating within countries under totalitarian regimes waged a battle for human rights, freedom of expression, and self-determination. The Solidarity movement in Poland, led by Lech Walesa, exemplifies the power of solidarity, as workers and intellectuals joined forces in a nonviolent struggle against the communist regime. Their collective resistance ultimately led to the fall of the Iron Curtain and the dismantling of oppressive systems in Eastern Europe.

The United States witnessed a powerful civil rights movement in the mid-20th century, as African Americans and their allies resisted racial segregation and demanded equal rights. Led by figures such as Martin Luther King Jr., Rosa Parks, and Malcolm X, these nonviolent resistance efforts brought attention to the systemic racial injustices faced by African Americans. They paved the way for significant legal and social reforms.

Simultaneously, the feminist movement emerged globally, calling for gender equality and challenging societal patriarchal structures. Women's rights activists raised their voices against discrimination, wage disparities, and the denial of basic rights. The struggle for gender equality proved to be a powerful force for change, reshaping societal norms and galvanising diverse movements for women's rights worldwide.

The Digital Age and Evolving Forms of Resistance:

With the advent of the digital age, resistance found new

avenues of expression and mobilisation. Digital platforms and social media networks have become powerful tools for organising and amplifying voices of resistance. Movements such as the Arab Spring in the early 2010s highlighted the ability of ordinary individuals to come together, coordinate actions, and challenge oppressive regimes through social media platforms. Activists used technology to share information, raise awareness, and mobilise mass demonstrations, leading to significant political upheaval in countries such as Egypt, Tunisia, and Syria.

In addition to digital platforms, art and culture have also emerged as potent forms of resistance in the modern era. Artists and creatives have used their work to challenge social norms, provoke thought, and spark conversations about pressing issues. Whether through visual art, music, performance, or literature, culture can inspire, unite, and instigate change.

Furthermore, resistance is not limited to specific periods or geographical locations. It is a perennial force that continues to shape our world today. From the fight against racial injustice and police brutality to the struggle for Palestinian rights to the battle against climate change, resistance movements persist and evolve.

Conclusion:

Resistance is a thread that weaves through the tapestry of human history, connecting struggles and movements across time and space. From ancient civilisations to the present day, resistance has been a catalyst for change, enabling individuals and communities to challenge oppression, defy unjust systems, and fight for a better future. The stories of resistance remind us of the power of collective action, the strength of the human spirit, and the enduring desire for freedom, justice, and equality. As we examine these narratives of resistance, we are encouraged to reflect upon our own roles in shaping a more just and equitable world.

2

Ancient Civilisations and the Birth of Resistance

Resistance has been a constant companion throughout the vast expanse of human history, a thread intricately woven through the ages. We find traces and flourishing examples of defiance against oppressive rulers and unjust systems, even in the earliest civilisations. Exploring the origins of resistance in the annals of ancient history is a journey that unfolds like a mesmerising epic, filled with tales of bravery and unwavering determination.

One of the earliest examples of resistance can be found in Mesopotamia, also known as the "Cradle of Civilisation." The Sumerians, the forefathers of human civilisation, boldly rebelled against their rulers here. As early as 2350 BCE, the Sumerian city-states revolted against Sargon of Akkad's hegemony, which sought to centralise power and impose his authority with an iron fist. The Sumerian King List, an ancient chronicle etched on clay tablets, also reveals numerous instances where city-states valiantly resisted foreign dominance over the centuries.

However, resistance in ancient Mesopotamia was not limited to political rebellion. The Sumerians, known for their advanced civilisation, expressed their resistance through the lyrical beauty of their literary works. The renowned "Lament for Ur," a Sumerian poem that mourns the tragic fall of the majestic city of Ur to the marauding Elamites, is one such example that has stood the test of time. The Sumerians expressed their sorrow and indomitable spirit of defiance, refusing to let the flames of their culture die out. Indeed, preserving their culture was an act of resistance in and of itself, a determined effort to preserve their identity amid conquest's tumultuous chaos.

Ancient Egypt, steeped in the grandeur of its pharaohs, witnessed acts of resistance, especially during the reigns of those mighty rulers. The timeless story of Moses leading the Hebrews out of Egypt is a testament to the power of resistance. Shackled by the chains of slavery and oppressed by Pharaoh's tyranny, the Israelites dared to confront their oppressors' colossal might. While the story contains mythical elements, it serves as an indelible reminder of the unwavering spirit of resistance against tyranny that prevailed even in ancient history's hallowed corridors. The Israelites' resistance was not limited to a physical struggle for liberation; it embodied a profound spiritual and cultural rebellion against their oppressors' yoke, a hymn of defiance that echoed through the sands of time.

When we look at ancient Greece, we see a society that was celebrated for its democratic ideals but where resistance flourished. Greek city-states rose in unison within this progressive civilisation, a symphony of defiance against the spectre of tyrannical rulers, their voices harmonising to preserve their democratic traditions. The most celebrated of these episodes is the Athenian resistance against the formidable Persians during the tumultuous Greco-Persian Wars. The very essence of democracy was intertwined with the spirit of resistance here. The Greek city-states, united by their fervent love of freedom and unyielding thirst for autonomy, took up arms against overwhelming odds to defend their cherished way of life, etching their collective determination into the annals of history and providing an enduring wellspring of inspiration for future generations of resistance movements.

However, resistance in ancient Greece went beyond mere political revolts. The philosophical schools that flourished during this golden age, such as the Cynics, Stoics, and Epicureans, can be seen as intellectual resistance movements. Thinkers like Diogenes of Sinope, Zeno of Citium, and Epicurus emerged as intellectual rebels. They dared to question societal norms and rulers' unchecked authority and advocate for a virtuous life free of external constraints. Their teachings echoed themes of personal freedom, self-reliance, and the never-ending pursuit of happiness, providing individuals with an alternative way to resist the shackles of social injustice and oppression.

In ancient Rome, the establishment of the Roman Republic opened avenues for resistance to oppressive aristocrats and would-be dictators. Shakespeare's dramatic portrayal of Julius Caesar's assassination by a group of senators, immortalised in history, can be seen as a poignant act of resistance against his burgeoning autocratic tendencies. During Rome's transition from a republic to an empire, subjugated peoples staged numerous uprisings, each motivated by a strong desire to reclaim their freedom and assert their rights. The Jewish revolts against Roman rule, particularly the First and Second Jewish Revolts, stand out as significant chapters in the history of resistance, fuelled by a complex mix of religious zeal, nationalism, and socio-political motivations.

Nonetheless, the tapestry of resistance stretches far beyond the borders of Mesopotamia, Egypt, Greece, and Rome. Throughout human history, resistance has emerged in various civilisations worldwide. History presents a rich mosaic of resistance against exploitation and tyranny, from indigenous tribes in the Americas who valiantly resisted the tide of European colonisation to ancient Chinese peasants who rose in defiance against oppressive feudal lords. The Mayan resistance to the juggernaut of Spanish conquest, the Tamil resistance to Chola imperialism in the sun-kissed lands of South India, and the Carthaginian defiance of Rome's relentless expansionist ambitions—all of these instances exemplify the indomitable human spirit that yearned for liberation, self-determination, and justice.

The emergence of resistance in these ancient civilisations was not limited to armed uprisings. Philosophers and thinkers emerged as a formidable force, challenging dominant ideologies and championing the cause of social transformation. Confucius' teachings in ancient China, as well as the revolutionary ideas of ancient Indian philosophers such as Buddha and Mahavira, are shining examples of resistance through the power of intellectual discourse. These visionary minds dared to challenge societal norms, scrutinised existing power structures, and presented alternative visions for a just and harmonious society.

Understanding the origins of resistance in these ancient civilisations provides profound insights into the seeds of dissent sown throughout human history. It is a lasting reminder that the fervent desire for freedom, justice, and autonomy is intrinsic to the human spirit. This timeless yearning has transcended time and space. These ancient acts of resistance paved the way for future generations to challenge oppressive systems and ardently strive for a better world, inspiring individuals to rise valiantly against adversity and carry the torch of resistance forward through time.

3

The Middle Ages: Religion and Resistance

During the medieval era, religion wielded an all-encompassing influence over societal affairs, exerting profound sway over politics, social dynamics, and intellectual discourse. Nevertheless, not all individuals submitted unquestioningly to this ecclesiastical dominion. Instead, they charted a course of resistance, mounting formidable challenges to the prevailing religious orthodoxy and endeavouring to redefine the intricate interplay between individuals and institutional entities.

Heresy emerged as one of the earliest manifestations of religious resistance during the medieval epoch. Heretical movements arose as dissenting voices vehemently opposed the teachings and practises sanctioned by the Catholic Church. For instance, consider the Cathars inhabiting the lush landscapes of southern France. They espoused a dualistic cosmology, contending that the material realm bore the imprints of diabolical creation. Consequently, they disregarded numerous Catholic sacraments and rituals, ardently advocating for a more streamlined, spiritually-infused expression of Christianity.

Similarly, in the northern reaches of Italy, the Waldensians mounted a vociferous critique of the Church's opulent riches and hierarchical structure, exalting the virtues of austerity, humility, and the profound significance of direct engagement with scriptural texts. These disparate heretical movements precipitated a direct challenge to the ecclesiastical hegemony of the Catholic Church and its monopolistic control over theological interpretation. In response, religious authorities orchestrated the establishment of the Inquisition, an ecclesiastical tribunal dedicated to identifying, prosecuting, and eradicating heretical tendencies. The arsenal of the Inquisition encompassed an assortment of methodologies, including the harrowing practice of torture and the public spectacle of burnings at stake, all meticulously engineered to stifle dissent and perpetuate the Church's dominance. Nevertheless, despite the relentless endeavours devoted to this enterprise, heretical movements persisted, leaving an indelible mark on the tapestry of Europe's religious landscape.

One notable instance of religious resistance during the medieval epoch was the Protestant Reformation, a transformative phenomenon reverberating across both the religious and political realms. The genesis of this epoch-defining movement can be traced to the indomitable spirit of Martin Luther, a dedicated Augustinian monk whose efforts commenced in 1517. Luther directed his formidable intellectual prowess toward critiquing the sale of indulgences, contending that the salvation of souls rested solely on unwavering faith, untouched by the commercialisation of divine clemency. His Ninety-Five Theses swiftly ascended to the forefront of theological discourse, effectively kindling a conflagration of unparalleled intellectual enquiry and reformist fervour. However, Luther's polemical disquisitions transcended the confines of his initial critique, assuming the form of a multifaceted assault on various foundational tenets and practises endorsed by the Catholic Church. His interrogation of the Pope's ecclesiastical authority, emphasis on the universal priesthood of believers, and impassioned plea for individualised interpretations of scriptural texts ignited spirited debates. The advent of Johannes Gutenberg's revolutionary invention, the printing press, expedited the dissemination of Luther's ideas, propelling them across the European continent with unparalleled velocity, engendering spirited debates and kindling the collective fervour for reform. The Protestant Reformation gave birth to an eclectic array of Protestant denominations, each characterised by its unique theological predispositions and modes of resistance vis-à-vis the Catholic Church.

For example, the ecclesiastical landscape of Geneva was presided over by the indomitable John Calvin, who extolled the doctrine of predestination and envisioned a harmonious Christian society governed by the imperatives of religious rectitude. In contrast, consider the milieu of Zurich, where Huldrych Zwingli spearheaded a theological paradigm shift, advocating for a symbolic interpretation of the Eucharist while soundly rejecting transubstantiation. These eminent reformers, among an illustrious pantheon of others, broadened the horizons of Protestantism, thus propelling a vibrant diversity of religious ideologies into the crucible of European religious discourse, thereby catalysing an epoch marked by the coexistence and contestation of multiple religious paradigms.

However, the dissemination of Protestant ideas ignited a conflagration of religious wars and internecine conflicts that sundered the fabric of societies across the continent. The German Peasants' War, a confluence of socio-economic grievances and simmering religious discontent, erupted in the early 16th century, resulting in widespread insurrections against feudal overlords and ecclesiastical holdings. Subsequently, the annals of history bear witness to the protracted Wars of Religion that convulsed France, spanning multiple decades, as Catholic and Protestant factions waged a relentless struggle for dominance, inflicting grievous casualties and untold devastation in their wake.

The annals of history reveal a profound interplay between political machinations and religious resistance during the medieval epoch, as secular rulers artfully navigated the intricate labyrinth of ecclesiastical authority. The Investiture Controversy, an epochal conflict that unfolded during the late 11th and early 12th centuries, embroiled the Holy Roman Empire and the papal seat in an intractable struggle for supremacy in ecclesiastical appointments. Secular potentates, including the enigmatic Henry VIII of England, astutely discerned the potential of harnessing religious resistance as a potent tool to secure their autonomy and consolidate their spheres of influence. The rupture of Henry VIII's association with Rome and the subsequent establishment of the Church of England are indelible testaments to how political imperatives intermeshed with the currents of religious resistance, ultimately shaping the course of history.

The annals of the Middle Ages bear witness to innumerable instances of resistance against religious conventions and institutional norms, reflecting the multifaceted tapestry of medieval society. From heretical movements that castigated the Church's authority to the Protestant Reformation that catalysed a profound transformation of European Christendom to the intricate power struggles that unfurled between ecclesiastical leaders and secular rulers, the medieval epoch served as an incendiary crucible of religious and political metamorphosis. The legacy of these acts of resistance continues to animate our comprehension of religiosity, the dynamics of power, and the intricate interplay between individual agency and the edifices of institutional authority. They serve as a poignant reminder that the quest for religious autonomy and the reform of ecclesiastical institutions are perennial pursuits that demand incessant critical scrutiny and contemplation, even when confronted with the inexorable march of adversity.

4

The Enlightenment Era: Resistance as Intellectual Rebellion

During the epoch known as the Enlightenment, a fresh wave of resistance arose, a period spanning the 17th and 18th centuries that bore witness to a profound transformation in thought. This era was marked by a remarkable shift in intellectual paradigms that exalted reason while harbouring a streak of scepticism and a burgeoning devotion to individualism.

Within this chronological sphere, luminaries embarked upon the formidable endeavour of challenging the conventions of their day, the established authorities, and the oppressive systems that held sway. Their chosen arsenal consisted of ideas and the written word, as they aspired to liberate society from ignorance, superstition, and the dogmatic tenets of religion.

It is imperative to acknowledge that the resistance mounted by these Enlightenment intellectuals transcended mere political symbolism; at its core, it represented an intellectual odyssey to reconstruct society through the propagation of rationality, critical thought, and the ideals of egalitarianism.

Among the eminent figures of this era, one encounters Voltaire, the French philosopher and scribe who, under the birth name François-Marie Arouet, etched an indelible imprint upon the intellectual landscape. Voltaire's literary oeuvre advocated for religious tolerance, freedom of expression, and the unequivocal distinction between church and state.

Born in 1694, Voltaire bore witness to the stark realities and flagrant hypocrisies that the Catholic Church, monarchy, and aristocracy perpetuated. His campaign against religious intolerance and trenchant critiques of corrupt institutions marked him for censorship and persecution. He endured imprisonment on two occasions and eventual exile, yet he refused to be silenced. His literary compositions, including the celebrated opus "Candide," probed the inequities and power abuses that permeated society, all while issuing a clarion call for realising a more equitable and enlightened world. Voltaire's unwavering commitment to the pursuit of honesty and justice solidified his status as an emblem of resistance against tyranny.

Another towering luminary of this epoch was Jean-Jacques Rousseau, the Swiss-French philosopher and litterateur whose birth occurred in 1712. Rousseau embarked upon a formidable crusade against the established social and political orders of his era through his pioneering treatises on social contract theory and the inherent natural rights of individuals. In his seminal work, "The Social Contract," Rousseau posited that true political legitimacy could only emanate from the consensus of the governed, espousing the need for a government firmly rooted in the sovereignty of the populace. He levelled scathing censure against the absolute monarchy, advocating instead for a more egalitarian societal framework in which individual liberty coexisted harmoniously with the broader interests of the general will. His emphasis on the importance of the general will and the promulgation of the common good served as a wellspring of inspiration for revolutionary movements and played a pivotal role in establishing republican forms of governance.

The Enlightenment epoch also bore witness to the efflorescence of salon culture, wherein writers, thinkers, and intellectuals convened within the confines of private residences to engage in spirited and erudite intellectual discourse. These salons functioned as vibrant hubs of resistance, furnishing a platform for exchanging radical ideas and serving as a potent counterpoint to entrenched conventions and institutions. Notably, women, in particular, occupied a pivotal role in hosting and participating in these salons, shattering societal constraints and becoming integral to the larger endeavour of fostering a more inclusive and progressive society.

Figures of note, such as Madame de Staël, Émilie du Châtelet, and Mary Wollstonecraft, actively championed feminist ideals, vociferously advocating for women's rights, access to education, and the pursuit of social equality.

Through their literary compositions and active participation in these intellectual gatherings, these women defied conventional gender norms, contributing significantly to the broader mission of cultivating a more inclusive and progressive society.

Moreover, the scientific revolution that unfurled during the Enlightenment epoch constituted a seminal contribution to intellectual resistance. Visionaries such as Isaac Newton, Galileo Galilei, and René Descartes assailed long-cherished beliefs about the natural world, effectively paving the way for a new era of scientific enquiry and rational thought.

Newton's groundbreaking principles of motion and universal gravitation, Galileo's audacious heliocentric model of the cosmos, and Descartes' rigorous method of doubt, accompanied by his unwavering commitment to reason, collectively wrought a sea change in the landscape of scientific thought.

These advancements engendered a novel worldview that fundamentally challenged established authority and underscored the primacy of empirical evidence as the bedrock of truth.

The empowerment of scientific thought dovetailed seamlessly with the overarching objectives of the Enlightenment, fostering an environment wherein individuals felt emboldened to interrogate prevailing paradigms, scrutinise entrenched dogma, and disentangle themselves from oppressive systems.

This intellectual rebellion transcended politics, permeating the realm of knowledge and heralding an era characterised by profound scientific and philosophical advancement. It is worth noting that the Enlightenment epoch transcended geographical confines, exercising its influence on thinkers and catalysing resistance on a global scale.

In the American context, luminaries such as Thomas Paine and Benjamin Franklin played pivotal roles in shaping the American Revolution. They vociferously advocated for independence and the establishment of a democratic republic. Paine's influential pamphlet, "Common Sense," mounted a direct challenge to the authority of the British monarchy, igniting widespread support for American independence.

Franklin's scientific experiments, diplomatic endeavours, and prolific literary output underscored the formidable potential of enlightened thinking in pursuing political and social transformation. The ideals of individual rights, liberty, and self-governance germinating during the Enlightenment became foundational principles for the United States and other post-colonial nations, profoundly shaping the trajectory of modern history.

However, it is imperative to recognise that the Enlightenment epoch, notwithstanding its lofty ideals of liberty, equality, and reason, was not devoid of its own flaws and contradictions. While it fervently championed the ideals of the Enlightenment, it frequently marginalised certain segments of society, including women and enslaved individuals, within its discursive ambit and its vision of a more equitable society. Paradoxically, many Enlightenment thinkers, while extolling the virtues of liberty, remained complicit in perpetuating systems of oppression, including but not limited to slavery, colonialism, and gender and racial disparities. These darker facets of the Enlightenment's legacy serve as a stark reminder that intellectual resistance, even when animated by noble ideals, remains susceptible to the biases and limitations inherent to its historical milieu. Recognising these contradictions and the ongoing struggles for comprehensive inclusion and equality remains imperative to our understanding of contemporary societies.

Nevertheless, the intellectual rebellion of the Enlightenment epoch laid a robust foundation for subsequent movements and revolutions, profoundly influencing the course of modern history. The Enlightenment thinkers and litterateurs passionately championed critical thought, the acknowledgement of individual rights, and the relentless pursuit of knowledge as core tenets of democratic societies. Their enduring legacy attests to the transformative potential of ideas and the capacity of individuals to mount a challenge against oppressive systems through intellectual discourse, thereby reshaping prevailing norms and advocating for meaningful social and political change. This legacy finds expression in the development of democratic governance, the advancement of human rights, and the ongoing quest for knowledge and scientific progress, all of which continue to delineate the contours of contemporary society.

5

XIXth Century: The Age of Revolutions and Nationalism

The 19th century marks a transformative epoch characterised by a significant shift in societal dynamics and the rise of revolutionary ideologies. Commencing with the unfurling of the French Revolution in 1789, Europe bore witness to a seismic transformation that would indelibly shape the course of history for decades to come. Spanning over a decade, the French Revolution encapsulated a tumultuous era that not only dismantled an age-old monarchy but also gave birth to enduring principles of liberty, equality, and fraternity, resonating deeply with individuals across the globe. This revolution was propelled by profound discontent among the

French populace, who shouldered the burdens of feudalism, economic disparities, and political oppression. As the monarchy crumbled, so did the conventional social order, ushering in a new era of revolutionary ideals.

The French Revolution reverberated far beyond France's borders, inciting individuals and communities throughout Europe to challenge oppressive regimes and wholeheartedly embrace the concept of self-determination. Its principles and rallying cries, including "liberty, equality, fraternity," echoed across the continent, offering solace and inspiration to those yearning for autonomy from despotic rule. These echoes of the French Revolution transcended national boundaries, igniting fervent nationalist movements that sought emancipation from colonial powers and attaining national sovereignty.

Across Europe, nations such as Greece, Belgium, and Poland passionately fought for independence against imperial forces. In the Americas, Latin American nations rose in defiance against Spanish and Portuguese colonisers, setting in motion a wave of decolonisation. Nationalism emerged as a dominant force in the 19th century, leaving an indelible mark on political and cultural landscapes.

The sense of belonging to a specific nation, steeped in shared history, traditions, and language, served as a unifying element for people striving to assert their identity against external influences. During this period, music, literature, and art emerged as potent expressions of nationalism, reflecting a people's distinctive cultural heritage and fostering a collective sense of pride and belonging. The ascendancy of nationalism generated debates concerning the demarcation of national boundaries and the nature of political allegiance. Some championed ethnically homogeneous nation-states, advocating for the self-determination of distinct cultural groups.

In contrast, others embraced more inclusive notions of civic nationalism, wherein the bond among citizens transcended ethnicity. These debates and conflicts over national identity would continue to shape political discourse for years. Beyond the political and social manifestations of nationalism, the 19th century bore witness to the emergence of potent ideological movements, each offering alternative blueprints for societal transformation. Liberalism, upheld by luminaries like John Stuart Mill and Alexis de Tocqueville, extolled individual rights, limited government intervention, and the pursuit of personal freedom. Socialism, born of mounting inequality and working-class exploitation, clamoured for economic equity and wealth redistribution. Simultaneously, the radical ideology of communism, embodied by Karl Marx and Friedrich Engels, advocated for the abolition of private property and the establishment of a classless society.

Resistance against oppressive regimes during this epoch assumed multifarious forms. While armed uprisings, such as the European Revolutions of 1848, manifested in certain regions, political protests, intellectual discourse, and dissemination of revolutionary ideas through publications and secret societies exerted an equivalent influence.

Subterranean networks, like the Carbonari in Italy and the Young Europe movement, endeavoured to coordinate revolutionary activities and foster solidarity among like-minded souls. The impact of the Age of Revolutions and nationalism in the 19th century proved profoundly transformative, fundamentally altering the trajectory of history. The principles and aspirations that emanated from these movements laid the groundwork for developing modern democracies and challenged entrenched power structures. Additionally, these revolutionary fervours redrew borders, dismantled colonialism, and ushered in the birth of new nations.

The 19th century stands as an enduring testament to the indomitable spirit of humanity and its unwavering quest for freedom, justice, and equality. The legacies of the Age of Revolutions and nationalism persist, continuing to shape the contemporary world, reminding us of the potency of resistance, and inspiring us to strive for a more equitable and just society. As we navigate the complexities of the modern era, it remains incumbent upon us to contemplate the lessons of the past and forge a future that upholds the ideals of liberty, equality, and fraternity for all.

6

Colonial Resistances: The Struggle for Identity and Autonomy

The era of colonialism witnessed a myriad of resistance movements across the globe as oppressed populations waged formidable battles against the imposition of foreign dominion and the denial of their inherent rights. These movements stemmed from an ardent yearning for self-determination, preserving cultural identities, and the unwavering pursuit of autonomy.

In Africa, Asia, and the Americas, indigenous peoples and enslaved populations confronted European powers and their colonial apparatuses with unyielding mettle and determination. They resolutely opposed colonisers' exploitative practices. They ardently fought for their independence while striving to safeguard their cultural heritage and reclaim their sense of self.

These resistance movements manifested in diverse forms, spanning from armed insurrections to peaceful protests and nonviolent acts of defiance, each reflective of the distinct circumstances and aspirations of the communities involved. One notable instance of colonial resistance was witnessed during the American Revolution, where the thirteen colonies mounted a challenge to British rule and ardently pursued sovereignty. Galvanised by Enlightenment ideals and the concept of individual liberty, the trailblazers of this revolution engaged in a relentless struggle to forge a new nation unburdened by the yoke of colonial dominion. Through acts of defiance, such as the Boston Tea Party and the signing of the Declaration of Independence, the American Revolution established a precedent for other movements against colonial powers, serving as an inspirational wellspring and a poignant testament to the possibility of resisting oppression.

In India, the indomitable Mahatma Gandhi emerged as a seminal figure in the battle for independence from British rule. Employing nonviolent resistance, civil disobedience, and peaceful acts of protest, Gandhi and his adherents sought to preserve their cultural identity and secure autonomy for their nation. The Indian independence movement, with its iconic Salt March and the Quit India Movement, assumed the mantle of hope and resilience, influencing other anticolonial movements on a global scale. Gandhi's principles of nonviolence and his emphasis on the spiritual and moral facets of resistance served as a wellspring of inspiration for generations of activists worldwide.

Africa also witnessed many decolonisation movements as nations across the continent waged fervent battles for their emancipation. Leaders such as Kwame Nkrumah in Ghana, Jomo Kenyatta in Kenya, Amílcar Cabral in Guinea-Bissau and Cape Verde, Patrice Lumumba in Congo, and Nelson Mandela in South Africa fervently championed the liberation and self-determination of their people. These leaders galvanised their communities to oppose the oppressive policies of colonial powers. They vociferously advocated for the restoration of their cultural and political autonomy. They envisioned Africa as an independent nation and a united continent, nurturing the spirit of Pan-Africanism and championing African unity in the face of persistent exploitation and marginalisation.

In the Americas, resistance against European colonialism assumed diverse forms as well. Indigenous populations in Canada, the United States, and Latin America valiantly resisted land dispossession, forced assimilation, and cultural obliteration. From the resilient struggles of the Apache, Cherokee, and Sioux in the United States to the enduring efforts of the Mapuche in Chile and the Aymara in Bolivia, indigenous communities grappled with formidable challenges in their quest to safeguard their lands and ways of life. The indigenous rights movements in these regions fervently sought recognition of their rights, the preservation of their cultural heritage, and the protection of their ancestral lands. The activism of indigenous leaders such as Eddie Mabo in Australia, Rigoberta Menchu in Guatemala, and Wilma Mankiller in the United States played an instrumental role in raising awareness about the ongoing injustices faced by indigenous peoples and fostering global solidarity.

Colonial resistance extended beyond physical confrontations; it encompassed intellectual and cultural movements. Writers, artists, and intellectuals were pivotal in nurturing a sense of identity and a fervent desire for autonomy among colonised populations. Through their literary and artistic expressions, they contested the dominant colonial narratives. They celebrated the rich cultural heritage and history of their people. These cultural and intellectual contributions emerged as potent forms of resistance, offering alternative perspectives and narratives that countered the dehumanising portrayal of colonised populations. Several influential writers emerged during this epoch of colonial resistance, significantly contributing to the anti-colonial discourse.

Frantz Fanon, an Afro-Caribbean psychiatrist and philosopher, delved into the psychological ramifications of colonialism in his seminal work "The Wretched of the Earth." He contended that the struggle for national liberation and cultural identity necessitated not only political resistance but also a profound process of psychological decolonisation. Fanon's writings called for a radical reevaluation of social, political, and cultural constructs, urging individuals to reclaim their agency and challenge the internalised oppression imposed by colonial powers. His works continue to inspire activists and intellectuals across the globe.

Similarly, Aimé Césaire, a Martinican poet and politician, in his groundbreaking work "Discourse on Colonialism," offered a critique of colonialism as a system rife with violence and dehumanisation. Césaire spotlighted the perniciousness of colonial ideologies and advocated for the repudiation of Western hegemony. His articulations of resistance and decolonisation resonated deeply within colonised communities, providing a conceptual framework for comprehending how colonisation permeated every facet of existence and the pressing imperative to dismantle colonial structures. Through his political activism and writings, Césaire emerged as a prominent figure in the Négritude movement, which sought to reclaim African and African diasporic cultural identities.

In addition to these intellectual contributions, cultural expressions of resistance, including literature, music, and art, played a pivotal role in asserting cultural identities and nurturing a sense of autonomy. For instance, during the Harlem Renaissance of the 1920s, African-American writers, poets, and musicians celebrated their cultural heritage and confronted prevailing racial hierarchies. Langston Hughes, Zora Neale Hurston, and Duke Ellington embraced their African roots. They showcased the richness of Black culture, laying the groundwork for subsequent generations to pursue cultural affirmation and transcend the constraints imposed by a white-dominated society. Their artistic creations emerged as potent tools for challenging stereotypes and affirming the worth and dignity of African-American experiences, influencing the broader civil rights movements that would unfold in the ensuing decades.

While these resistance movements yielded profound impacts, their struggles did not conclude with the formal cessation of colonial rule. Numerous nations continue to grapple with the enduring legacies of colonialism, endeavouring to reclaim their cultural practices, revitalise their languages, and assert their rights on the global stage. Ongoing initiatives to decolonise education, address historical injustices, and preserve cultural heritage remain pivotal in asserting autonomy and fostering a more equitable world.

In summation, colonial resistances constituted multifaceted struggles for identity and autonomy. These movements galvanised individuals and communities united by an unwavering resolve to reclaim their liberty and assert their entitlement to self-determination. The repercussions of these resistances reverberate across time, shaping the post-colonial world and standing as a testament to the indomitable spirit of humanity. Intellectual and cultural contributions further enriched the anti-colonial discourse, challenging colonial ideologies and nurturing a sense of pride and resilience within colonised populations. These collective endeavours continue to influence the ongoing process of decolonisation and the assertion of cultural identities in the contemporary world. The struggles of the past inform the present, serving as a poignant reminder of the significance of empathy, comprehension, and solidarity as we navigate the complexities of our shared global history.

7

The World Wars: Resistance Against Occupiers and Tyrants

The commencement of the World Wars during the 20th century ushered in vast devastation and profound anguish while simultaneously giving birth to a myriad of forms of resistance against both occupiers and despots. In this chapter, we explore the valiant acts of defiance that unfolded during this tumultuous epoch in history. We examine the diverse strategies employed by individuals and collectives in their audacious endeavour to challenge the tyrannical regimes that sought to impose their dominion.

1. Resistance in Territories under Occupation:

World War I and II witnessed the occupation of numerous nations by hostile forces. Within these occupied domains, resistance movements emerged driven by an unwavering commitment to safeguard national identity, defy military subjugation, and strive toward emancipation. These movements adopted a multifarious array of tactics, spanning from the art of guerrilla warfare and acts of subversion to the establishment of covert networks and the art of intelligence procurement. During the span of World War II, the French Resistance, known as La Résistance, emerged as an emblem of unyielding opposition to Nazi occupation. This resistance effort encompassed a tapestry of diverse groups and individuals comprising both genders. Their endeavours encompassed acts of bombing, targeted assassinations, and acts of sabotage, all while providing indispensable intelligence to the Allied forces. The disruptive impact of their actions on German military operations was profound, bolstering civilian morale and paving the way for the eventual liberation of France.

2. The Role of Subterranean Networks:

Subterranean networks played a pivotal role in underpinning resistance endeavours during the epoch of the World Wars. These clandestine networks served as sanctuaries of refuge, hubs for creating counterfeit documentation, conduits for the clandestine transportation of vital supplies, and orchestration centres for acts of subversion. The individuals who undertook these perilous missions risked their existence in the relentless pursuit of intelligence gathering, thus ensuring the success of resistance undertakings. Within the context of World War II, the Zegota organisation epitomised the potency of subterranean networks. Zegota, signifying the "Council to Aid Jews," engaged in an unwavering mission to effect the rescue of Jewish individuals and provide them with shelter, sustenance, and fabricated identification credentials. Guided by a diverse cadre of activists, intellectuals, and religious leaders, Zegota managed to preserve the lives of thousands of Jewish individuals, a testimony to the remarkable valour and solidarity exhibited even in the face of dire personal risk.

3. *Partisans and the Art of Guerrilla Warfare:*

Partisan collectives and guerrilla combatants clandestinely operated behind enemy lines, orchestrating a series of ambushes, wreaking havoc upon vital infrastructure, and mounting acts of sabotage that disrupted military operations. These champions of resistance exhibited an aptitude for unorthodox stratagems, adroitly adapting to the distinctive challenges presented by their environments and sowing seeds of trepidation within the hearts of the occupying forces. The Yugoslav Partisans, under the stewardship of Josip Broz Tito, waged an unrelenting guerrilla campaign against Axis forces during World War II. Hailing from the remote enclaves of mountains and densely forested regions, the Partisans undertook daring hit-and-run assaults, severing critical supply lines and conscripting fighters from an eclectic spectrum of backgrounds. Their unyielding resistance served to immobilise substantial enemy resources and played a pivotal role in the battle against Nazi occupation within the Balkan territories.

4. Rebellions within the Confines of Concentration Camps:

In the face of unfathomable horrors, incarcerated individuals within concentration camps meticulously choreographed acts of insurrection. These acts, ranging from meticulously orchestrated uprisings to isolated manifestations of defiance, were executed to preserve human dignity, inflict harm upon their captors, and kindle flames of hope within an otherwise bleak existence. One particularly salient instance is the Warsaw Ghetto Uprising of 1943. Confronting the spectre of deportation and extermination, the Jewish residents of the Warsaw Ghetto mounted an armed insurrection against the Nazi forces. Despite being overwhelmingly outnumbered and outgunned, these valiant fighters tenaciously held their ground for an extended period, inflicting substantial casualties upon the German troops. Their unflinching resistance was a poignant testament to their indomitable resolve to oppose oppression. It served as an inspirational beacon, catalysing subsequent uprisings within other Nazi concentration camps.

5. Resistance from Within the Ranks of Occupying Forces:

It is a historical verity that not all individuals serving within occupying forces did so with unswerving compliance to the oppressive regimes they represented. A clandestine cadre of individuals within these occupying forces covertly aligned themselves with the resistance movements, thereby providing invaluable intelligence, engaging in acts of subterfuge, and assisting the local populace. These manifestations of resistance from within the very bosom of the enemy's ranks exerted a transformative influence, ultimately contributing to the erosion of the occupiers' endeavours. Within the precincts of the German military establishment, a diminutive assemblage known as the White Rose emerged as a paragon of valour in their battle against Nazi despotism. Comprising predominantly of university students and their erudite professors, they clandestinely disseminated anti-Nazi missives, imploring their compatriots to defy Hitler's autocratic regime. Notwithstanding the severe reprisals they endured, including the execution of several members, their actions attested to the capacity for resistance to materialise from the most unexpected quarters. Even within the crucible of totalitarianism, these resolute individuals embodied the capacity of a few intrepid souls to challenge the status quo.

6. Resistance Against Tyranny:

The World Wars bore witness to resistance movements

that arose to challenge tyrants who sought to consolidate their dominion within their nations. These movements took shape as bulwarks against autocratic rule, the propounding of fascist ideologies, and the stifling of civil liberties. In Italy, where the Fascist regime of Benito Mussolini held sway, the Italian Resistance materialised as a formidable adversary to his authoritarian governance. Comprising a diverse panorama of ideological perspectives and political affiliations, the Italian Resistance undertook acts of sabotage, the art of intelligence acquisition, and the execution of guerrilla warfare. Their actions were instrumental in weakening Mussolini's stranglehold on power, thereby contributing to the eventual liberation of Italy by the Allied forces.

7. *Civil Disobedience and the Art of Nonviolent Resistance:*

Not all expressions of resistance during the World Wars manifested in armed confrontations. Civil disobedience and the art of nonviolent resistance emerged as influential modalities for challenging oppressive regimes. From strikes and protest demonstrations to clandestine publications and subversive literary endeavours, these expressions of resistance sought to erode the authority and legitimacy of tyrannical regimes. In the context of British colonial rule in India, Mahatma Gandhi harnessed the power of nonviolent resistance to contest the dominion of the British colonial apparatus and fervently advocated for Indian independence. Through acts of civil disobedience, such as the Salt March and the Quit

India Movement, Gandhi laid bare the oppressive nature of colonial rule and galvanised millions to join the struggle for emancipation. His modus operandi of nonviolence became an omnipotent instrument for resistance movements worldwide.

8. *The Integral Role of Women in the Tapestry of Resistance:*

The active participation of women inexorably enriched the panorama of resistance movements during the World Wars. From their engagement in espionage and service as couriers to their vital contributions to intelligence acquisition and the nursing of wounded combatants, women made a resounding impact, showcasing their mettle and courage in the face of adversity. Their contributions were indubitably pivotal in determining the outcomes of numerous resistance operations. Within the precincts of the Soviet Union, an untold multitude of women rallied to the banner of the partisan struggle, fighting shoulder-to-shoulder with their male counterparts against the encroaching tide of German invaders. The Night Witches, an exclusively female aviation regiment, executed daring nocturnal bombing sorties that sowed terror within the hearts of their adversaries. The feats of individuals such as Lyudmila Pavlichenko, a sniper whose tally of confirmed kills numbered an astounding 309, and Zoya Kosmodemyanskaya, an iconic martyr of the Soviet partisan movement, bore testimony to the profound impact of women within the tapestry of resistance.

IN CLOSING:

The World Wars were epochs marked by profound human suffering. However, they also witnessed extraordinary acts of resistance against occupiers and tyrants. From the clandestine networks and guerrilla warfare to the art of nonviolent resistance and the indomitable contributions of women, resistance emerged as an indomitable force that left an indelible imprint upon the course of global conflicts. The valour and sacrifices of those who resisted serve as a resounding testament to the unquenchable spirit of humanity when faced with the spectre of oppression.

8

The Cold War and Beyond: Ideological Resistances

The Cold War era, from the end of World War II to the early 1990s, was a period of significant global tension between two superpowers: the United States and the Soviet Union. This era was characterised by ideological conflict as nations, groups, and individuals opposed the dominant ideologies of communism and capitalism.

One of the prominent forms of ideological opposition during the Cold War was anti-communism, which manifested in various ways. In the United States, for instance, the government launched an extensive campaign known as the Red Scare, targeting individuals suspected of communist sympathies. This resulted in the persecution and blacklisting of many writers, actors, and artists considered subversive or a threat to American values.

The anti-communist sentiment in the United States was fueled by apprehension and anxiety over the spread of communism, especially following the communist victory in China in 1949 and the onset of the Korean War in 1950. In response, the US government implemented aggressive measures to root out suspected communist influence. The House Un-American Activities Committee (HUAC) initiated investigations into alleged communist activities, subjecting individuals to interrogations and compelling them to testify against their colleagues. This atmosphere of fear and suspicion had a chilling effect on freedom of expression and stifled dissent.

Similarly, within the Soviet Union and its satellite states, dissidents emerged as a potent force of ideological resistance. These individuals, often referred to as dissident writers, artists, and intellectuals, challenged the oppressive nature of the communist regime through their creative works. They utilised literature, art, and underground publications to express their dissent and reveal the realities of life in the Soviet bloc.

One notable figure in this movement was Alexander Solzhenitsyn, a renowned Russian writer and Nobel Laureate. Solzhenitsyn's works, including "One Day in the Life of Ivan Denisovich" and "The Gulag Archipelago," exposed the horrors of the Soviet Gulag system and the repression faced by ordinary citizens under the communist regime. Solzhenitsyn's writings were a powerful indictment of the Soviet system, sparking international discussions on human rights abuses and inspiring others to speak out against the regime.

In addition to individual acts of resistance, the Cold War witnessed larger ideological resistances, such as decolonisation movements in former colonies. Across Asia, Africa, and Latin America, many nations fought against their colonial oppressors, seeking independence and self-determination. These movements were often motivated by ideological principles, as colonised populations sought to free themselves from the dominance of Western capitalist powers.

Frantz Fanon, a psychiatrist and writer from Martinique, played a notable role in the decolonisation movement. His seminal work, "The Wretched of the Earth," eloquently depicted colonisation's psychological and physical effects on the colonised. Fanon argued that true liberation from colonial oppression required a complete rejection of the coloniser's culture and values. His ideas profoundly influenced liberation movements worldwide, inspiring activists to embrace revolutionary violence to overthrow their oppressors.

Furthermore, the Cold War era also witnessed the rise of countercultural movements that rebelled against mainstream ideologies. The 1960s and 1970s saw protest movements advocating for civil rights, gender equality, and opposition to war. These movements, often fueled by values of freedom, peace, and social justice, aimed to challenge prevailing power structures and establish alternative systems based on equality and justice.

In the United States, the Civil Rights Movement, led by influential figures like Martin Luther King Jr. and Malcolm X, sought to dismantle systemic racism and achieve equal rights for African Americans. Their nonviolent protests and powerful speeches galvanised the nation and forced it to confront deep-seated prejudices. Similarly, the feminist movement, led by prominent figures such as Gloria Steinem and Betty Friedan, challenged gender norms and fought for women's rights, leading to significant societal shifts in attitudes toward gender equality.

As the Cold War drew close, ideological resistance continued to shape the world. The collapse of the Soviet Union created new opportunities for resistance movements, both within the former communist states and globally. Non-governmental organisations (NGOs) and human rights activists emerged as crucial advocates for social justice, democracy, and freedom of expression.

The post-Cold War era strengthened transnational movements as activists addressed global issues such as climate change, poverty, and corporate power. For instance, the anti-globalisation movement critiqued neoliberal capitalism's impacts and called for more equitable economic systems. The World Social Forum, a gathering of activists and organisations worldwide, provided a platform for exchanging ideas and strategies to challenge dominant economic and political structures.

Technological advancements, particularly the internet and social media rise, further facilitated ideological resistance. Digital platforms offered new avenues for dissent, enabling individuals and groups to mobilise, share ideas, and challenge dominant narratives. Movements like the Arab Spring and Occupy Wall Street demonstrated the power of digital resistance in mobilising populations and demanding change.

The Arab Spring, a series of uprisings across the Middle East and North Africa, was primarily driven by social media platforms like Facebook and Twitter. These platforms allowed individuals to organise protests, disseminate information, and rally support for their cause. The self-immolation of Tunisian street vendor Mohamed Bouazizi, in protest of government oppression, symbolised resistance and inspired a wave of uprisings in the region.

Similarly, the Occupy Wall Street movement began in 2011 and used social media to amplify voices protesting economic inequality and corporate influence in politics. The movement's critique of the "1%" and calls for economic justice resonated globally, leading to similar movements in other countries.

The Cold War and its aftermath represent critical periods of ideological resistance. They shaped the political, cultural, and social landscapes of nations worldwide. Ideological resistance during this time was not confined to a single ideology or geographic location but rather a complex tapestry of interconnected movements and individuals challenging the status quo and striving for a more just and equitable world.

In this chapter, we have explored the various forms of ideological resistance that emerged during the Cold War and examined how these resistances continue to shape our world today. We have delved into the lives and works of key figures, analysed the impact of technological advancements on resistance movements, and discussed the enduring legacy of ideological resistance in the 21st century. From the literary dissidents who exposed the repressive nature of the Soviet regime to the activists fighting for social justice in the digital age, the spirit of resistance and the pursuit of a better world remain as potent as ever.

The Cold War era also witnessed forms of ideological resistance beyond politics and social justice. Artists and intellectuals played a vital role in challenging dominant cultural and artistic norms, pushing the boundaries of creativity and self-expression. The avant-garde movement emerged as a force of resistance against traditional artistic conventions, seeking to disrupt established norms and explore new artistic possibilities.

Artists such as Pablo Picasso, Salvador Dali, and Jackson Pollock embraced unconventional forms, abstract expressionism, and surrealism to create works that challenged traditional notions of beauty and representation. Their art often mirrored the Cold War era's chaos and uncertainty, reflecting the time's anxieties and contradictions.

Picasso's famous painting, "Guernica," is a powerful testament to the horrors of war and the suffering inflicted on innocent civilians. Created in response to the bombing of the town of Guernica during the Spanish Civil War, the painting depicts the brutality and destruction of war, capturing the pain and anguish of the victims. "Guernica" became a symbol of anti-war sentiment and a powerful tool for resistance against the violence and aggression of the time.

Similarly, in literature, writers like Samuel Beckett and Albert Camus challenged conventional narrative structures and explored existential themes. Beckett's play, "Waiting for Godot," embodies the absurdity of human existence and the futility of waiting for salvation or meaning in a chaotic world. On the other hand, Camus explored the themes of existentialism and the search for meaning in his novel, "The Stranger." These literary works defied the conventions of storytelling and questioned the foundations of human existence, resisting the prevailing ideologies of the Cold War era.

Beyond art and culture, religion and spirituality were also arenas of ideological resistance during the Cold War era. Religious leaders and movements played vital roles in advocating for peace, justice, and human rights, challenging the dominant narratives of the superpowers.

One example is the Civil Rights Movement in the United

States, where prominent figures like Martin Luther King Jr. and other religious leaders utilised the power of faith and moral principles to advocate for racial equality. Their resistance against racial discrimination was grounded in the belief in the inherent dignity and worth of every individual, regardless of their race or background.

Similarly, in Latin America, the Liberation Theology movement emerged as a strong force of resistance against social and economic inequalities. Influenced by Marxist ideas and the teachings of Jesus, Liberation Theology sought to address poverty, injustice, and oppression, advocating for the rights of the poor and marginalised. Figures like Archbishop Oscar Romero of El Salvador became iconic symbols of resistance and solidarity.

The Cold War era and ideological tensions created fertile ground for resistance in various forms and arenas. Behind the veil of politics and global power struggles, individuals, writers, artists, religious leaders, and activists all found ways to challenge the dominant ideologies and strive for a more just and equitable world.

While the specific contexts and forms of resistance have evolved since the end of the Cold War, the spirit of ideological resistance continues to shape our world today. The fight against injustice, inequality, and oppression remains as relevant now as it was during the Cold War era. From grassroots movements advocating for climate justice to activists calling for racial equality and gender liberation, the legacy of ideological resistance is alive and thriving.

The Cold War era serves as a reminder of the power of ideas and the transformative potential of resistance. It reminds us that in the face of dominant ideologies and oppressive systems, individuals and communities can challenge the status quo and work towards a more inclusive and just society.

As the world continues to grapple with new challenges and ideologies, it is crucial to draw inspiration from the history of ideological resistance and learn from the strategies and tactics employed by those who came before us. By studying the movements, individuals, and ideas that resisted the dominant ideologies of the Cold War era, we can gain insight into the power of collective action, the importance of solidarity, and the necessity of challenging unjust systems.

The legacy of ideological resistance during the Cold War era calls on us to remain vigilant, to question prevailing narratives, and to challenge oppressive systems wherever they exist. It serves as a reminder that change is possible and that pursuing a more just and equitable world is a continuous struggle that requires ongoing resistance, resilience, and imagination.

9

Modern Era: Digital Revolutions and The Power of Information

In the contemporary era, we have witnessed an unparalleled transformation in the manifestation of resistance. The advent of the digital age, coupled with the ascent of the internet and mass communication technologies, has revolutionised how individuals organise and articulate their dissent.

The potency of information has wrought a metamorphosis upon the terrain of resistance movements, reconfiguring the dynamics of activism and confronting established power structures. With a click of a button, individuals can now disseminate their ideas globally, reaching audiences hitherto inconceivable. This newfound accessibility has democratised resistance, amplifying marginalised voices and catalysing a fresh wave of grassroots movements. Social media platforms have evolved into formidable instruments for mobilising kindred spirits, orchestrating coordinated actions, and raising awareness regarding injustices transcending borders. The ease with which information, images, and videos can be shared online has proven instrumental in drawing attention to systemic issues and facilitating collective action. Noteworthy examples include hashtags like #BlackLivesMatter, #MeToo, and #FridaysForFuture, which have ignited international dialogues, galvanised support, and pressured institutions to address systemic problems.

One of the most conspicuous instances of this modern-day resistance is the Arab Spring, a series of uprisings that swept through the Middle East and North Africa in 2011. Protesters harnessed the power of social media platforms such as Twitter and Facebook to orchestrate demonstrations, disseminate real-time information, and expose government corruption. This unprecedented technology deployment enabled the rapid dissemination of information, dismantling traditional communication barriers and challenging entrenched power structures.

Furthermore, the repercussions of the digital revolution extend beyond social movements. It has fundamentally reshaped how individuals seek and consume information. Historically, sources of news and information were subject to the control of a select few gatekeepers, such as newspapers, television networks, and publishing houses. However, the ascent of the internet has democratised access to information, ushering in a wide spectrum of sources and perspectives.

This democratisation of information has had profound ramifications for resistance movements.

Activists can now access alternative news sources, grassroots blogs, and independent journalism, all offering nuanced perspectives often absent in mainstream media. Consequently, resistance movements have become better informed and interconnected, fostering a deeper comprehension of the issues and a more robust capacity to challenge prevailing narratives. Furthermore, the internet has facilitated the formation of virtual communities characterised by shared interests and objectives. Online platforms enable individuals to forge connections and collaborate with like-minded individuals, creating global networks of solidarity. These digital communities provide emotional support, share resources, and amplify each other's messages, cultivating a sense of belonging and empowering individuals to take decisive action. The capacity to access information effortlessly and instantaneously has also empowered citizens to hold governments and institutions accountable.

Whistleblowers, exemplified by figures such as Edward Snowden, have harnessed the internet as a tool to expose covert surveillance programmes and infringements on privacy perpetrated by intelligence agencies. The release of classified documents initiated a global discourse on the balance between security and individual rights, ultimately leading to reforms and enhanced transparency in certain nations. Moreover, the digital age has engendered novel forms of resistance, including hacktivism and cyber warfare. These unconventional tactics involve computer technology to disrupt or unveil systems and networks perpetuating injustice.

From activist hackers targeting oppressive regimes to state-sanctioned cyberattacks, the digital sphere has transformed into a battleground for ideological confrontations and power dynamics. However, it is imperative to acknowledge that the digital age presents challenges. While the internet has opened up new avenues for resistance, it has simultaneously introduced fresh obstacles. Governments and corporations have employed surveillance technologies to monitor and regulate online activities, curtailing dissent and infringing privacy. The dissemination of counterfeit news and disinformation campaigns has also eroded the credibility of online information, rendering it increasingly arduous to distinguish veracity from manipulation.

In this contemporary era, resistance transcends the confines of physical protests, demonstrations, or offline activism alone. The influence of information and the digital revolution has ushered new prospects for individuals and groups to challenge authority, foster societal transformation, and shape public opinion. The digital realm has become integral to contemporary resistance, facilitating global connections, amplifying voices, and mobilising efforts to pursue a more just and equitable world. As we navigate this ever-evolving digital landscape, we must subject our actions to rigorous scrutiny, ensuring our resistance remains anchored in the relentless pursuit of justice, truth, and freedom. The power of information, while transformative, necessitates responsible utilisation, ethical considerations, and an unwavering commitment to nurturing inclusive and diverse online spaces. By harnessing the potential of the digital age, we can continue to push the boundaries of resistance, challenge oppressive systems, and forge a brighter future for all.

10

Resistance in Arts and Culture

Art has always been an unwavering bastion, steadfastly standing as a powerful medium for expressing dissent, a platform for challenging the prevailing status quo, and a source of profound inspiration for resistance. Its enduring relevance resonates across the annals of history, where artists and cultural luminaries have harnessed their creative talents to illuminate the shadows of social injustice, dissect the intricacies of political inequities, and lay bare the stark realities of economic disparities. In doing so, they have catalysed introspection, nurtured spirited discourse, and ignited the flames of change and transformation.

Within the framework of this discourse, we delve ever deeper into the labyrinthine nuances of the role of resistance in the realm of arts and culture, seeking to not only spotlight but also unravel the manifold forms and mediums through which artists, visionaries, and creatives alike have waged valiant battles against the spectre of oppression, wielding their pens, brushes, voices, and imaginations as potent weapons in the ceaseless struggle for a fairer, more equitable world.

The realm of visual arts stands as a citadel of resistance, where creative minds have wielded the mighty brushstroke and the evocative image as formidable weapons in their arsenal. From the biting satire of political cartoons that pierce through the armour of oppressive systems to the clandestine acts of graffiti artists who dare to scrawl messages of dissent on the walls of conformity, visual artists have fearlessly embraced the canvas as a battleground of ideas. Iconic works such as Pablo Picasso's haunting "Guernica" serve as indelible testimonies to the horrors of war, the unrelenting suffering of civilians, and the collective resolve to resist the looming spectre of fascism. Nevertheless, the power of resistance extends beyond the realm of the visible, as the lens of photography has also been harnessed to chronicle pivotal moments, document the fervour of protests, and expose the raw nerve of injustices to the gaze of the world. The indomitable image of the lone "Tank Man" standing defiantly before a column of armoured vehicles during the tumultuous Tiananmen Square protests of 1989 stands as an enduring symbol of resistance against the iron fist of authoritarianism.

However, the canvas of resistance in the visual arts extends far beyond explicit political statements.

Symbolism and metaphors have, time and again, been employed as nuanced forms of resistance, where artists such as Frida Kahlo and Diego Rivera have deftly wielded surrealist techniques and vivid symbolism to raise consciousness regarding personal struggles, the gross abuses of human rights, and the harrowing plight of indigenous communities. This approach transcends the boundaries of mere political commentary, allowing their art to become a universal language that speaks to the hearts and minds of individuals from diverse backgrounds, transcending the boundaries of nations and cultures.

Literature, too, unfurls as a rich tapestry interwoven with threads of resistance. Renowned authors such as George Orwell, through masterpieces like "1984," have skillfully employed the medium of fiction to serve as cautionary tales, sounding the alarm against the perils of totalitarianism and championing the primacy of individual freedom. By conjuring vivid and often dystopian visions of the future, these literary luminaries have offered readers a stark mirror to examine the potential consequences of unchecked power, serving as beacons of vigilance against the creeping shadows of authoritarianism. Similarly, authors such as Chinua Achebe, Arundhati Roy, and Toni Morrison have lent their pens and voices to amplify the narratives of marginalised communities, shining an unrelenting spotlight on issues ranging from colonialism and racism to gender inequality.

Their eloquent prose and unflinching narratives have acted as catalysts for social change, urging readers to question the established norms, challenge the existing paradigms, and take up the mantle of justice. In music, the harmony of resistance has often served as a powerful unifying force in times of tumultuous change. Protest songs have emerged as anthems for movements, their lyrics carrying the collective hopes, aspirations, and demands of a generation seeking justice and equality. From the heartland of the civil rights movement in the United States, where anthems like "We Shall Overcome" echoed through the streets, to the distant shores of South Africa, where iconic figures like Miriam Makeba and Hugh Masekela used their music as a call to action in the fight against apartheid, melodies have become the beating heart of social transformation. Genres like hip-hop, reggae, and folk music have transcended the boundaries of entertainment, serving as platforms for marginalised communities to articulate their grievances, voice their aspirations, and demand a reckoning with the entrenched systems of injustice. Performance arts, too, have etched their mark on the canvas of resistance, providing a hallowed stage for the voices of the marginalised to reverberate with unyielding clarity.

Theatre, dance, and performance art have served as crucibles for questioning societal norms, the scrutiny of authority, and the exposure of the fault lines within oppressive systems. The works of pioneering playwrights such as Bertolt Brecht and Augusto Boal have embraced techniques such as epic theatre and forum theatre to engage audiences on a visceral level, prodding them to question the status quo and interrogate the social and political structures they often take for granted. For instance, Brecht's concept of alienation sought to dismantle the illusion of realism in theatre, compelling audiences to cast a critical eye on the constructs of their societies.

In the digital age, resistance within arts and culture has adopted new forms, seizing the potential of social media platforms, podcasts, and online art exhibitions as arenas for creative expression and societal transformation. Online movements such as #BlackLivesMatter and #MeToo have witnessed the extraordinary power of digital spaces, where voices once silenced or marginalised find resonance, organising protests and catalysing change. Moreover, the frontiers of virtual and augmented reality technologies have continued to expand, providing artists with innovative tools for immersive storytelling. These technologies enable artists to craft experiences that immerse audiences in the stark realities of oppressed communities, fostering empathy and motivating action.

Artists and cultural icons have persistently occupied the vanguard of resistance movements. Their unwavering courage, boundless creativity, and unyielding determination to confront the established order have inspired generations and initiated conversations that have steered momentous social and political metamorphoses. Through the tapestry of their artistry, they have underscored a profound truth: that resistance extends beyond the realm of physical confrontation and is manifest through the boundless realms of imagination, creativity, and the art of storytelling. However, the path of resistance within arts and culture has its challenges and tribulations. Artists often find themselves pitted against the forces of censorship, repression, and even violence as the consequences of their bold expressions. Governments and authorities, keen on preserving their dominion, may seek to stifle dissenting voices, viewing art as a potent threat to their hegemony. Throughout history, numerous artists have faced persecution, imprisonment, or been compelled into exile due to the audacity of their defiant works. However, it is through their resilience and their steadfast commitment to their artistic vision that they continue to inspire others to resist, to rise against the tide, and to champion justice.

Furthermore, resistance within arts and culture does not always receive unanimous acclaim. Certain works may ignite controversy, provoke criticism, and even incite backlash from those at odds with the conveyed messages. Artists grapple with navigating the turbulent waters of societal divisions, addressing multifaceted issues, and striking a delicate balance between stirring thought and potentially alienating audiences. Paradoxically, these contentious works often lead to the most profound dialogues and the most transformative conversations and compel society to confront uncomfortable truths. For resistance within arts and culture to truly take root and wield its full transformative potential, it necessitates the active engagement of audiences. Through dialogue, introspection, and decisive action, the seeds of resistance sown by artists can flourish into tangible change. Audiences are beckoned not merely to consume passively but to actively listen, participate, question, and remain open to the challenges posed by the established norms. In doing so, they become indispensable allies in the resistance movement, amplifying the voices of artists and ushering in a more just, equitable, and enlightened society.

In summation, resistance within the arts and culture emerges as a formidable and enduring force that transcends epochs. Artists, visionaries, and creatives, driven by an unwavering commitment to challenging oppressive systems, kindling change, and providing a resounding voice for the marginalised, continue to employ their talents as a catalyst for conversation, a force for disrupting established narratives, and a beacon of hope that ignites the fervour of resistance. By scrutinising the multifaceted tapestry of resistance within the arts, we understand how creativity can serve as a potent instrument for change in the world. This exploration of resistance within the arts and culture is an enduring testament to the indomitable power of human expression and the relentless pursuit of justice and equity.

11

The Philosophy of Resistance in the 21st Century

In the 21st century, the concept of resistance has undergone a significant evolution, encompassing a diverse range of philosophical perspectives and methodologies. It extends far beyond its traditional boundaries, now encompassing intellectual, social, and cultural dimensions alongside physical acts of defiance. This chapter delves into the intricate landscape of resistance philosophy, offering insights into its response to the intricate challenges posed by the modern world.

One prominent philosophy of resistance in the 21st century is post-structuralism, championed by eminent thinkers such as Michel Foucault and Judith Butler. These scholars have fearlessly challenged conventional power structures and ideologies, emphasising the imperative to resist dominant discourses perpetuating inequality and oppression. According to them, resistance involves unveiling and deconstructing the concealed power dynamics that quietly shape our existence.

Foucault's influential concept of power-knowledge underscores the interplay between power and knowledge production within society. He posits that power is not merely imposed upon individuals but intricately woven into social institutions and practices. Consequently, resistance necessitates a profound examination and subversion of these structures of power knowledge, challenging established norms and revealing covert mechanisms of control. Foucault also delves into the notion of counter-conduct, which involves subversive acts and tactics capable of disrupting and challenging the normalising power of institutions. Through counter-conduct, individuals can resist and construct alternative modes of existence.

Butler's groundbreaking concept of gender performativity expands the realm of resistance, particularly concerning matters of sexuality and gender identity. She posits that gender is not an inherent category but rather a social construct performed by individuals. In this context, resistance involves disrupting and defying normative gender roles, affirming the validity of diverse gender identities. By refusing to conform to societal expectations, individuals disrupt the power dynamics that uphold oppressive gender norms. Furthermore, Butler underscores the importance of collective action and solidarity within resistance movements, emphasising that marginalised groups can draw strength and support from collective resistance against oppressive structures.

Another significant philosophical perspective in the realm of resistance is existentialism. Existentialist philosophers like Jean-Paul Sartre and Albert Camus underscore the importance of individual freedom and authenticity as the foundation of resistance. They contend that resisting societal pressures and expectations necessitates individuals embracing their autonomy and taking responsibility for their actions.

Sartre's concept of radical freedom posits that individuals are not mere products of external circumstances but possess the power to transcend them through their choices. According to Sartre, resistance entails asserting one's freedom and actively engaging in actions aligned with one's values and beliefs. By claiming their subjectivity, individuals resist being reduced to objects or products of their circumstances. Sartre also delves into the ethics and responsibility associated with resistance, highlighting the importance of considering the impact of one's actions on others and society as a whole.

Camus, on the other hand, delves into the philosophical exploration of the absurd in a seemingly chaotic and irrational world. He argues that individuals must confront the absurdity of existence and actively rebel against it. This rebellion involves rejecting meaninglessness and striving for personal integrity and authenticity within a universe devoid of inherent purpose. Camus introduces the concept of the rebel, an individual who resists in the face of adversity and refuses to accept the absurd as the ultimate truth. The rebel's resistance is not necessarily aimed at achieving a specific goal. However, it serves as an affirmation of human dignity and a defiance against absurdity.

Moreover, the philosophy of resistance in the 21st century

extends its reach to encompass environmentalism and ecological resistance. With the growing awareness of climate change and the degradation of natural habitats, many philosophers argue that resistance must now encompass the protection of our planet. Environmental activists, inspired by thinkers like Vandana Shiva and Arne Naess, advocate for a profound connection with nature and the imperative to resist human actions that harm the environment.

Shiva's ecofeminist philosophy underscores the intersectionality of environmental and gender-based oppressions. She contends that the exploitation of nature is intrinsically linked to the exploitation of women, both stemming from a patriarchal and capitalist worldview that prioritises profit over the well-being of people and the Earth. In this context, resistance involves forging alternative ways of living that challenge the dominant paradigm, emphasising ecological sustainability and gender equity. Shiva also highlights the significance of traditional ecological knowledge and indigenous wisdom in guiding resistance movements and promoting sustainable practices.

Naess introduces the concept of deep ecology, advocating for a fundamental shift in the human-nature relationship from dominance to deep interconnectedness and respect. Deep ecologists argue that resistance lies in recognising the intrinsic value of all life forms and promoting ecological citizenship. This calls for individuals to actively strive to protect and restore ecological systems through personal and collective action. Naess also emphasises the importance of self-realisation and personal transformation in cultivating a deep ecological consciousness that informs resistance to environmental degradation.

Additionally, the rise of technology and the digital age has given birth to new forms of resistance. Online activism and hacktivism have become potent tools for challenging authority and championing social justice. From the Arab Spring to the Occupy Wall Street movement, social media and digital platforms have played a pivotal role in mobilising resistance and amplifying the voices of marginalised communities.

Activists and thinkers, exemplified by the cyberphilosopher Alexander Galloway, analyse how various forms of power exploit digital networks. They argue that resistance in the digital age necessitates the disruption and subversion of the control exerted by governments and corporations over information flows and online spaces. Hacktivist groups like Anonymous embody this resistance by exposing corruption and advocating for transparency, blurring the boundaries between the virtual and physical realms. Galloway also explores the concept of radical transparency as a form of resistance wherein individuals and organisations challenge the surveillance and control mechanisms of powerful entities.

Furthermore, the 21st century has witnessed the rise of intersectional resistance. This philosophy recognises the interdependence of various forms of oppression and calls for collective action against multiple systems of domination. Intersectional resistance emphasises the importance of addressing issues related to race, gender, class, and other identity axes in creating meaningful and effective resistance movements.

Drawing from the work of scholars like Kimberlé Crenshaw and Bell Hooks, intersectional resistance challenges the tendency to prioritise a single issue or identity over others. It underscores the necessity of recognising and addressing how different forms of oppression intersect and compound one another. By embracing intersectionality, resistance movements can foster solidarity and inclusivity, dismantling the hierarchical structures perpetuating injustice. Crenshaw also explores the concept of intersectional feminism, which centres on the experiences and voices of marginalised women within resistance movements.

Overall, the philosophy of resistance in the 21st century mirrors our world's dynamic and ever-changing nature. It acknowledges that resistance manifests in diverse forms and is not bound by any particular ideology or methodology. As we navigate the complexities of our time, philosophers and activists continually explore fresh avenues for challenging the status quo and advocating for a more just and equitable world. The philosophies discussed in this chapter provide a robust foundation for comprehending and engaging in resistance, whether through intellectual critique, social activism, environmental stewardship, or the use of technology. By integrating these diverse perspectives and embracing intersectionality, individuals and communities can work towards transformative change and liberation from oppressive power systems.

12

Resistance in Literature

Resistance in literature has perennially emerged as a multifaceted and recurring theme, consistently inspiring and intellectually challenging readers throughout the annals of literary history. From the narratives of antiquity to contemporary works of fiction, the world of literature has been an instrumental domain for authors to effectively portray various manifestations of resistance against prevailing structures of oppression, societal norms, and injustices. This chapter delves into a comprehensive examination of the profound significance of resistance within the literary sphere, encompassing an exploration of its historical contextualisation, the psychological impact it imparts upon its readers, and its profound transformative potential in reflecting and actively shaping societies.

1. THE LITERARY MEDIUM AS A VEHICLE FOR RESISTANCE:

Throughout epochs, literature has remained a formidable platform that provides writers with the agency to express dissent, challenge established paradigms, and question the status quo. The narrative canvases that authors employ serve as illuminating portals into the ordeals confronted by marginalised individuals and communities, effectively fostering empathy and engendering a heightened social consciousness amongst its readership. By juxtaposing alternative perspectives and subjecting existing power structures to critical scrutiny, literature effectively equips individuals to question prevailing norms and articulate their own voices when confronting adversities. Over the course of history, literary creations have emerged as instrumental agents of transformative change, serving as catalysts for catalysing discourse, shaping public opinion, and galvanising movements that seek to usher in social reform.

2. ARTISTIC PORTRAYAL OF INDIVIDUAL ACTS OF RESISTANCE:

One of the captivating attributes inherent to literature is its capacity to vividly depict the unwavering tenacity displayed by individuals who defy societal expectations and challenge established norms. These literary figures stand as luminous exemplars of courage and determination, beckoning readers to reassess their beliefs and values critically.

The literary landscape is replete with a diverse spectrum of characters who boldly challenge conventions, ranging from the indomitable spirit of Antigone in Sophocles' iconic play to the tenacious resilience embodied by Huckleberry Finn in Mark Twain's renowned novel. These literary personas, through their internal conflicts, struggles, and eventual triumphs, effectively transcend their fictional realms to become beacons of inspiration, emphasising that a solitary individual can exert a profound influence and potentially catalyse broader movements for change. Literature inherently motivates its audience to scrutinise authority, combat injustices, and ardently pursue their authentic selves by enabling readers to identify with these characters.

3. COLLECTIVE RESISTANCE AND REVOLUTIONS:

While literature frequently delves into individual resistance, it also offers invaluable insights into the dynamics of collective resistance and the transformative potential of revolutions. Literary works such as George Orwell's "1984" and Aldous Huxley's "Brave New World" serve as cautionary tales, underscoring the perils of totalitarian regimes and emphasising the imperative of challenging authority. These dystopian narratives illuminate the consequences of acquiescence to conformity and underscore the vital necessity of collective action against oppressive governments. Additionally, literary masterpieces such as Aleksandr Solzhenitsyn's "One Day in the Life of Ivan Denisovich" and Ayn Rand's "Atlas Shrugged" lay bare the arduous struggles of individuals contending with oppressive political, economic, or social systems. Through their masterful storytelling and evocative portrayals, authors amplify the voices of marginalised groups, elicit empathy from their readers, and expose the atrocities perpetrated by authoritarian rulers, motivating individuals to take a principled stand against injustice.

4. LITERATURE AS A CATALYST FOR SOCIETAL TRANSFORMATION:

Over time, literature has been duly recognised as a potent instrument for facilitating transformative societal change. By laying bare societal injustices and systemic deficiencies, novels, plays, and poetry have consistently challenged deep-seated prejudices, stoked public discourse, and instigated tangible reforms within society. Harriet Beecher Stowe's "Uncle Tom's Cabin," a seminal work of the 19th century, significantly catalysed the abolitionist movement, awakening public consciousness to the profound iniquities inherent to slavery. Similarly, Upton Sinclair's "The Jungle" was a stark exposé of unscrupulous practices within the meatpacking industry, leading to substantial regulatory reforms and enhanced labour conditions. These illustrative examples amply demonstrate the formidable capacity of literature to function as an agent of reform, wielding considerable influence in shaping public sentiment, eliciting collective action, and subsequently reshaping society for the better.

5. RESISTANCE IN THE CONTEXT OF IDENTITY:

Within the realm of literature, the intricate interplay between resistance and identity emerges as a thematic construct of immense import. It furnishes readers with the opportunity to scrutinise the tribulations endured by individuals who steadfastly endeavour to safeguard their cultural, ethnic, or gender-based identities. In Chinua Achebe's seminal work, "Things Fall Apart," readers are confronted with the tumultuous collision between the traditional values held by the African protagonist and the inexorable encroachment of colonialism. Through its portrayal of identity conflicts, literature serves as an illuminating lens, offering insights into prevailing power dynamics, entrenched prejudices, and the systematic marginalisation faced by minority communities and individuals. The literary work of Virginia Woolf, particularly "A Room of One's Own," courageously challenges patriarchal norms while exploring the repercussions of societal oppression on women's artistic expression and intellectual autonomy. These narrative explorations serve to underscore the paramount significance of self-determination, individual agency, and the indispensable role of communal support in resisting dehumanising forces. By artfully capturing the complexities associated with identity conflicts, literature encourages readers to critically assess and transcend societal constraints, thereby fostering inclusivity and celebrating the rich tapestry of human experiences.

6. LITERATURE'S ROLE IN FOSTERING EMPATHY AND CONNECTION:

Resistance as a central theme in literature actively fosters empathy by affording readers the opportunity to forge a profound connection with characters who confront oppression or resistance. Through their immersion in the narrative, readers acquire a heightened understanding of the myriad challenges marginalised individuals and communities encounter. This deepened empathy not only engenders a recognition of privilege but also serves as a powerful motivator, propelling readers towards action in the struggle against injustice and advancing societal change. Literature provides a communal space where connections are formed and shared experiences are embraced, transcending barriers and inspiring readers to confront their biases.

CONCLUSION:

The theme of resistance within the realm of literature stands as an instrumental medium for critique, empowerment, and catalytic change. The diverse narratives and compelling characters within the literary canon consistently challenge readers to interrogate prevailing ideologies, confront injustices, and envision a more equitable world. By embracing the thematic concept of resistance within the literature, we gain insights into historical struggles and actively participate in shaping a future characterised by inclusivity, justice, and compassion. Literature remains an indomitable instrument for resistance, beckoning readers to engage in an ongoing dialogue concerning societal transformation. Its potency resides in its ability to evoke empathy, nurture critical thinking, and galvanise collective action, making literature an indispensable companion in the quest for a more equitable and enlightened society.

13

Conclusion

Throughout this extensive study, we have delved deep into the complex realm of resistance and its significant impact on human societies across history. From the earliest civilisations to the present day, resistance has consistently emerged as a powerful force, moulding the path of our shared human journey. It stands as a determined opponent to oppressive systems, guiding us towards the principles of liberty, fairness, and equal rights, leaving an enduring imprint on our historical narrative.

As we explored the complex concept of resistance, we realised that it takes on various forms and motivations. It can appear as large-scale political movements, brave armed uprisings, nonviolent protests that bring about significant change, or individual acts of rebellion - each one proving the indomitable human spirit. Ultimately, resistance embodies the innate refusal to accept injustice, accompanied by an unshakable desire for a more just world.

Throughout history, we witnessed the emergence of numerous resistance movements in response to many oppressive forces. One of the most salient examples is the relentless struggle against the abhorrent institution of slavery. From the revolts of enslaved peoples in ancient Egypt, Greece, and Rome to the abolitionist movements of the 19th century, the battle against slavery resonates through the annals of time, leaving an enduring legacy in the pursuit of human dignity and equality.

Similarly, resistance against colonial rule paralleled the era of European expansion and dominance. Indigenous populations and colonised communities, spanning from the Aztecs and Incas in the Americas to the Maoris in New Zealand, valiantly fought to preserve their lands, cultures, and autonomy against the encroachments of foreign powers. This resistance assumed diverse forms, encompassing armed uprisings, guerrilla warfare, and political movements, all directed towards self-governance and independence.

The resistance against colonialism also reverberated through African, Asian, and Middle Eastern histories, culminating in the monumental struggles for decolonisation that gathered momentum in the mid-20th century. These movements challenged the stranglehold of European imperialism, ignited fervent nationalist aspirations, and ultimately birthed new nations. Visionaries such as Kwame Nkrumah, Jomo Kenyatta, and Ho Chi Minh led their nations in resolute resistance against colonial powers, inspiring generations and establishing a legacy of steadfast resilience and determination.

The Palestinian resistance against Zionist colonialism stands as a robust and enduring struggle that endures into the contemporary era. Rooted in the historical context of Zionist colonialism, characterised by externally imposed ideologies seeking dominance within Palestinian territories, this resistance movement emerged as a direct response to colonisation. It is marked by remarkable persistence and resilience in the face of ongoing challenges, constituting a complex and dynamic phenomenon. A critical examination of the Palestinian resistance reveals intricate dynamics at play. Politically, it encompasses organised movements employing diverse strategies, including armed struggle, diplomatic endeavours, and grassroots mobilisation, all aimed at resisting the encroachment of Zionist colonialism. Socio-culturally, it draws upon narratives of identity, heritage, and collective memory to foster unity and determination among Palestinians in their quest for self-determination. Furthermore, the endurance of this resistance in the 21st century underscores its significance as one of the few remaining struggles against colonialism on the global stage. This remarkable survival positions Palestine as a poignant case study within the discourse of postcolonialism. Consequently, comprehending the complexities inherent in the Palestinian resistance necessitates an interdisciplinary approach that combines historical analysis with sociopolitical examinations, all while recognising its broader implications for global anti-colonial movements.

The fight against oppression extends beyond the confines of political systems; it permeates the realms of social and cultural domains. For instance, the women's suffrage movement serves as a testament to the power of resistance in dismantling patriarchal structures and advocating for gender equality. Tireless activists like Susan B. Anthony, Emmeline Pankhurst, and Simone de Beauvoir challenged the notion that women were second-class citizens, steadfastly demanding their right to vote, work, and be treated as equals.

Resistance has also been intricately linked with struggles for civil rights and racial equality. From the African American freedom fighters during the civil rights era in the United States to the anti-apartheid movement in South Africa, people of colour have risen against systematic discrimination and racial oppression. Visionaries such as Martin Luther King Jr., Nelson Mandela, and Rosa Parks stand as symbols of courage and resilience, embodying the spirit of those who resisted and offering hope in the struggle for justice.

Furthermore, the fight against authoritarian regimes and oppressive governments has consistently fuelled resistance movements worldwide. The heroic endeavours of individuals like Mahatma Gandhi, Vaclav Havel, and Aung San Suu Kyi have showcased the power of nonviolent resistance in challenging dictatorial rule and inspiring transformative change. Often referred to as "people power," these movements underscore that solidarity, perseverance, and the refusal to surrender to fear can triumph even against seemingly insurmountable odds.

While resistance has often been intertwined with political and social struggles, it also manifests as a potent force within art and culture. Artists, writers, and musicians have harnessed their creative expressions as resistance tools, boldly challenging established norms and provoking thought. Through literature, paintings, films, and music, luminaries such as

Frida Kahlo, James Baldwin, Ai Weiwei, Mahmoud Darwish, Ghassan Kanafani, Emile Habibi and Bob Dylan have exercised their freedom of expression to critique oppressive systems, advocate for marginalised communities, and ignite conversations that challenge the status quo.

In the 21st century, resistance has assumed new dimensions with the advent of technology and the widespread use of social media. Digital platforms have become hubs for organising, mobilising, and amplifying diverse voices in the relentless pursuit of positive change. Movements such as #MeToo, Occupy Wall Street, and Fridays for Future have harnessed the power of digital activism, transcending geographical boundaries and uniting people in their shared quest for justice, equality, and environmental protection.

However, our challenges in the present era are multifaceted and interlinked. The urgency of addressing climate change, economic inequality, systemic racism, and political polarisation necessitates even deeper and more collective forms of resistance. It compels us to forge alliances across different struggles and adopt a global perspective that recognises our shared responsibility in building a more sustainable, just, and inclusive world. As we conclude this profound exploration of resistance, it is imperative to acknowledge that its power resides not only in the actions and strategies undertaken but also in the unwavering resilience, determination, and hope it embodies. It serves as a poignant reminder that in the face of adversity and oppression, the indomitable human spirit remains unyielding, constantly striving to reclaim dignity, rights, and a brighter future. As we confront the formidable challenges of our time, let us draw inspiration from the enduring legacies of resistance throughout history and muster the courage to stand against injustice, amplify the voices of the marginalised, and construct bridges of understanding and empathy that span the breadth of humanity's shared journey.

14

Post-Scriptum: A Historical Account of Palestinian Resistance to Zionist Colonialism and Oppression, From 1947 to 2024.

1. Introduction

This analysis presents a unique and all-encompassing viewpoint on the persistent and unyielding resistance of the Palestinian people against the oppressive and dominating forces of Zionism throughout the extensive period ranging from 1947 to 2024, spanning nearly eight decades. The primary objective is to illuminate the unwavering struggle for self-determination and autonomy that the Palestinians have embarked upon while elucidating the diverse spectrum of defiance that has defined and moulded this everlasting conflict. Meticulously delving into historical events, pivotal social movements, and influential individuals, this meticulous examination endeavours to provide an enlightening and objective exploration of the intricate narrative surrounding Palestinian resistance, establishing a foundation for deep contemplation and extensive analysis.

1.1 BACKGROUND OF ZIONIST COLONIALISM

Grasping the pith of Palestinian resistance calls for an in-depth and comprehensive examination of the backdrop of Zionist colonial dominance, which has played a pivotal role in shaping the struggle for Palestinian rights. This segment aims to delve into the origins and incentives that have propelled the Zionist campaign, leading to the establishment of a Jewish state within the historic landscape of Palestine. By scrutinising significant historical events such as the Balfour Declaration, the British Mandate, and the substantial influx of Jewish immigrants into Palestine, we can uncover the complex and multifaceted foundations of the Palestinian fight against colonial dominion. Through meticulous analysis and a thorough understanding of the intricate historical framework, we can better understand the Palestinian resistance movement, its challenges, and its aspirations for a just and lasting solution.(Reinharz and Golani, 2020), (Loevy 2021).

1.2 PALESTINIAN STRUGGLE FOR INDEPENDENCE

The Palestinian crusade for sovereignty is a key focus of this comprehensive analysis. This portion presents an incredibly detailed and extensive overview of the hopes, objectives, and hurdles Palestinians encounter in their unwavering pursuit of self-governance. It meticulously traces the remarkable growth of Palestinian nationalism, examining the inception of diverse liberating bodies and the tireless application of militant resistance as a powerful medium to counter Zionist subjugation effectively. By thoroughly mapping the extensive route of the Palestinian independence movement's countless adversities and noble goals, we gain profound insight into the unparalleled tenacity, indomitable spirit, and unwavering persistence of a united and deeply steadfast community in the relentless pursuit of reclaiming their sacred and cherished native soil. This land is intricately woven into the very essence of their identity, culture, and existence. (Khalidi, 2020), (Abukmeıl, 2022).

2. Pre-1947: Seeds of Resistance

Before the year 1947, there was evidence of a powerful and resolute resistance against the oppressive forces of Zionistic colonialism among the Palestinian communities. Completely aware of the impending battle, the Palestinians took the initiative to unite politically and culturally to establish a solid foundation for their upcoming resistance. They worked diligently to form various societal and cultural groups, paving the way for creating informational channels and educational institutions that would nurture a deep sense of Palestinian national identity and consciousness. During this crucial period in history, a multitude of Palestinian nationalist movements came into existence, serving as the bedrock for an arduous and prolonged struggle for self-determination that would span numerous decades. (Dana, 2020), (Kayali, 2020).

2.1 EARLY PALESTINIAN NATIONALISM

During the pre-1947 era, nascent Palestinian nationalism began amassing speed and gaining momentum as Palestinians began to express their unwavering commitment to their national identity in steadfast defiance of the Zionist colonial endeavours that sought to suppress their aspirations and rights. The resounding call for Palestinian self-determination echoed through the minds and hearts of the Palestinian people as they yearned for autonomy and unity, envisioning a future where their collective voice would shape the destiny of their land. The foundations of Palestinian nationalism were intricately woven by visionary thinkers, eloquent writers, and impassioned political advocates whose unwavering determination and intellectual prowess paved the way for a profound awakening of the Palestinian spirit. Emphasising the utmost importance of self-rule and a unified Palestinian stance, these influential figures spurred a spirited revival that ignited a blazing fire within the hearts of the Palestinian population. Through their thought-provoking writings, powerful speeches, and tireless activism, they instilled a deep sense of belonging in the Palestinian people, fostering an unbreakable bond with their ancestral lands, cherished heritage, and cherished traditions. This steadfast connection catalysed nurturing and fuelling a potent communal spirit of resilience and unwavering determination as the Palestinian populace stood united in their steadfast resistance against the oppressive yoke of colonial ambitions. The flame of Palestinian nationalism burned ever brighter, illuminating the path towards a future of freedom, justice, and liberation, where the Palestinian people could finally reclaim their rightful place on the global stage. (Hurewitz, 2022) (Alqaisiya, 2023).

2.2 BRITISH MANDATE AND ZIONIST IMMIGRATION

From 1920 to 1948, Palestine, a region of great historical significance, fell under the control of The British Mandate. This arrangement indirectly encouraged the immigration of Zionists, thereby fuelling discord and defiance among the diverse population. As the flow of Jewish immigrants intensified, the Palestinian Arab community's anxiety about their demographic and political fate deepened, creating a sense of urgency and concern. The British, influenced by the Balfour Declaration, fervently supported the Zionist aspirations, resulting in a significant increase in Jewish settlements and a progressively larger acquisition of land. This influx of Jewish settlers, coupled with the expansion of their territory, inevitably sparked a strong and widespread resistance movement among Palestinians. This resistance was showcased through various forms of protest, such as powerful demonstrations, impactful work stoppages, and passionate political rallying against the colonial enterprise. It was during this pivotal time in history that Palestinians solidified their unyielding stance against Zionist intrusion and the controversial policy of the Mandate. The Palestinian people, recognising the importance of preserving their cultural heritage and national identity, stood united and unwavering in their determination to protect their land, rights, and future. This turbulent period marked a turning point in the struggle for self-determination and independence, catalysing the ongoing conflict that continues to shape the region today. Despite the challenges faced by the Palestinian Arab community, their resilience and determination to resist and fight for their rights remained unshaken. The struggle against Zionist policies and the British Mandate became deeply ingrained in the collective consciousness, paving the way for future generations to carry on the quest for justice, equality, and the establishment of an independent Palestinian state. The legacy of this tumultuous era serves as a stark reminder of the complex and deeply rooted issues plaguing the region. It highlights the need for a comprehensive and just resolution that upholds the rights and aspirations of all individuals involved while fostering a spirit of mutual understanding and coexistence. Only through genuine dialogue and a commitment to peace can the wounds of the past heal, and a brighter, more harmonious future be forged for the people of Palestine and the entire region. (Cohen, 2020) (Hyamson, 2022) (Cohen).

3. 1947-1949: The Nakba and the Birth of Resistance

From 1947 through 1949, a critical and momentous transition in the Palestinian chronicle unfolded, marked by a seismic event known as the Nakba, which painfully translates to "Catastrophe." During this tumultuous era, the United Nations introduced a Partition Plan aiming to cleave the land of historical Palestine into separate Jewish and Arab entities, thus setting the stage for an unprecedented chain of events. This blueprint, despite its purported intentions, unwittingly and tragically instigated the forcible dislocation and banishment of hundreds of thousands of Palestinians from their ancestral homes, resulting in unimaginable suffering, widespread ruin, and profound distress that reverberated throughout the entire region. The Palestinian populace, bound by a shared sense of longing for justice and an unwavering commitment to their fundamental human rights, responded to these grave human rights violations with a powerful and resolute defiance. Faced with the immense challenges brought about by Zionist settler-colonialism and domination, the people of Palestine rose as one, vowing to resist, persist, and ultimately reclaim their rightful entitlements, their cherished land, and their long-denied independence. Thus, while an undeniably tragic chapter in history, the Nakba became the catalyst that fuelled the birth of an indomitable and unwavering resistance movement. Firmly rooted in their steadfast determination, the Palestinian people embarked on a tireless journey to restore their territorial sovereignty, uphold their inherent dignity, and reestablish their rightful place in the world. This remarkable resistance movement served as a testament to the extraordinary resilience, unity, and fortitude of the Palestinian people, who refused to be silenced or marginalised. In this transformative and defining period of Palestinian history, the Nakba represented not only a catastrophic rupture but also a rallying cry for justice, an impassioned call to action that resonated across borders and inspired countless individuals worldwide. The struggle for liberation and self-determination became deeply intertwined with the pursuit of human rights and dignity, transcending geographical boundaries and igniting the flames of solidarity among all those who stood in solidarity with the Palestinian cause. Thus, the significance and legacy of the Nakba continue to reverberate to this day, actively shaping the ongoing Palestinian struggle for justice and their unwavering quest for a brighter future. As the Palestinian people persist in their tireless pursuit of freedom, equality, and the realisation of their inherent rights, the spirit of resistance instilled during the Nakba remains an undying flame, a beacon of hope that guides their unwavering will to endure, resist, and ultimately triumph over all obstacles. (Manna, 2022) (Juliana, 2023) (Saadah, 2021).

3.1 THE UN PARTITION PLAN AND PALESTINIAN DISPLACEMENT

The 1947 United Nations Partition Plan, a pivotal moment in history, left an indelible mark on the Palestinian population, resulting in an immense tragedy that forever altered their lives. This plan triggered an unprecedented wave of displacement and forced expulsion, casting countless Palestinians away from their ancestral lands, homes, and communities. The consequences of this traumatic event led to a dire humanitarian crisis, where Palestinians were forced to abandon their belongings and means of sustenance. As time has passed, the echoes of this coerced migration continue to resonate as Palestinians tirelessly strive for justice and the fundamental right to return to the place they once called home. The UN Partition Plan serves as a haunting symbol of the deep-rooted injustices inflicted upon the Palestinian people, concealed beneath the guise of Zionist advancement and the annexation of Palestine. The repercussions of this plan reverberate through the present era, reminding the world of the ongoing struggle for freedom, equality, and the restoration of Palestinian rights. (Imseis, 2021) (Pressman, 2020).

3.2 FORMATION OF PALESTINIAN LIBERATION ORGANISATIONS

In the aftermath of the Nakba, the institution of Palestinian Liberation Organisations offered pivotal assistance in structuring the revolt against Zionist colonialism and injustice. These entities surfaced as representatives for the entitlements of the Palestinians, striving towards national liberation and the rejuvenation of their homeland. The Palestinian Liberation Organisation (PLO), established in 1964, amalgamated diverse factions and embodied the communal ambitions of the Palestinians. Via their political, diplomatic, and militant resistance, these organisations garnered global attention to the Palestinian plight and pursued self-governance, justice, and the preservation of their rich historical heritage. By raising awareness through various international platforms and engaging in comprehensive grassroots movements, the Palestinian Liberation Organisations steadfastly worked towards uniting the global community in recognising the urgency of their cause, promoting peaceful coexistence, and endeavouring to achieve lasting peace and stability in the region. (Barakat and Amouri, 2022) (Irfan, 2020) (Darraj, 2020).

3.3 GUERRILLA WARFARE AND ARMED RESISTANCE

Faced with insurmountable adversities and unyielding oppression, Palestinians fervently sought refuge in the realm of guerrilla warfare and armed resistance as indispensable mechanisms to effectively contend against the relentless forces of Zionist imperialism. Amid this epoch, numerous highly equipped Palestinian factions courageously materialised, fearlessly participating in multifaceted resistant acts, resiliently fighting against Israeli military forces, and strategically challenging the establishment of illegal settlements. Notably, the valiant Palestinian fedayeen, known for their unwavering dedication, astutely employed an array of tactical approaches to contest the unlawful occupation effectively and to ultimately reclaim the sacred Palestinian terrain. By steadfastly employing guerrilla warfare tactics, their overarching intention was to skillfully destabilise the prevalent Israeli military hegemony, thereby firmly establishing and asserting Palestinian autonomy and self-determination. Through their untiring resolve and formidable resistance, these audacious movements were elevated to an indispensable status, forever leaving an indelible and profound imprint on the rich tapestry of the Palestinian resistance endeavour. (Barak aet al., 2023) (Hamdan, 2023).

4. 1950s-1960s: Solidifying Resistance

Throughout the 1950s and 1960s, Palestinian firmness and unwavering determination against the oppressive force of Zionist colonialism and persecution solidified as a plethora of distinct and resolute movements and associations emerged to bravely confront the unjust occupation that plagued their beloved homeland. Fuelled by an unyielding resolution to reclaim their ancestral territory, the Palestinian population ingeniously employed a multifaceted and well-rounded arsenal of strategies, including armed opposition, diplomatic approaches, and the powerful force of collective community activism. These tireless endeavours were not only aimed at augmenting global awareness and understanding of the Palestinian plight, but also at boldly challenging and dismantling the prevailing narrative that Zionist entities had tirelessly disseminated. Drawing strength from their indomitable spirit, Palestinians took proactive steps towards establishing covert networks, covert training camps, and the orchestration of daring undercover operations, vital elements in their relentless pursuit of empowerment and liberation. These clandestine efforts played an instrumental role in bolstering their resistance against oppression and setting the necessary groundwork for the battles and struggles that would follow in their fervent quest for justice. The tireless endeavours undertaken during this pivotal period in history laid the foundation upon which the Palestinian people would continue to build a powerful and unwavering resistance movement, fuelled by an unwavering determination and a collective spirit that could never be extinguished. (Samra and Qutami2020) (Kimmerling, 2020) (Khan, 2022).

4.1 REFUGEE CAMPS AND GRASSROOTS ACTIVISM

Refugee encampments were transformed into crucial hubs of community activism during the 1950s and 1960s as displaced Palestinians endeavoured to rally and coordinate their communities. Despite the austere conditions of the camps, the resilient occupants engaged in collective endeavours, passionately building an array of educational institutions, healthcare units, and community associations that catered to the needs of the diaspora. The strength of their activism within these camps proved to be instrumental in sustaining their resilience, promoting unity, and preserving the rich Palestinian national character that had been forcefully displaced. Through their determined efforts, these activists created spaces where historical recollections were shared, cultural traditions were celebrated, and the vibrant Palestinian narrative thrived. By meticulously passing down the stories of their ancestors, they ensured that future generations comprehended the complexities and ongoing nature of the conflict. Through these collective endeavours, the indomitable spirit of the refugee community was imprinted upon the sands of time, emphasising the crucial need for sustained resistance and the unwavering determination to reclaim a homeland that had been unjustly taken from them. (Dalal, 2022) (Plakans, 2021) (Fitili aet al.2020).

4.2 ROLE OF ARAB STATES IN SUPPORTING PALESTINIAN CAUSE

Arab nations had a significantly noteworthy and substantial influence in earnestly endorsing and championing the righteous Palestinian cause throughout the pivotal and transformative decades of the 1950s and 1960s. Fully cognisant and deeply appreciative of the vital and unbreakable bonds of camaraderie, these illustrious nations wholeheartedly dedicated themselves to providing extensive and substantial financial assistance, unwavering logistical backing, and resolute diplomatic support to the valiant and noble Palestinian opposition. In extraordinary unison, nations of immense power and historical significance, such as Egypt, Syria, and Jordan, firmly aligned themselves with the brave and resilient Palestinians, staunchly standing against the abhorrent and oppressive policies inflicted upon them by the insidious and relentless forces of Zionist oppression and colonisation. With indomitable resolve, these revered Arab nations proudly assumed the role of hosts for the distinguished and esteemed headquarters of the Palestine Liberation Organisation (PLO), furnishing them with a safe sanctuary to strategise, organise, and instigate their noble cause. Furthermore, in their unwavering commitment and dedication to the Palestinian cause, these remarkable Arab nations selflessly took it upon themselves to provide extensive military training and support, enabling and empowering the valiant Palestinian fighters to undertake and execute audacious armed operations against the formidable Israeli forces. In the face of overwhelming adversity, their unyielding support exemplified the unity of their commitment and their resolute intent to fiercely and unflinchingly oppose and counteract the continued and flagrant usurpation, annexation, and encroachment upon sacred Palestinian land and the inherent and inalienable rights and privileges of its courageous people.

4.3 RISE OF PALESTINIAN NATIONALISM AND IDENTITY

The 1950s and 1960s witnessed a remarkable and significant upsurge in Palestinian nationalism and collective identity, which served as a powerful response to the encroachment of Zionist colonialism and the oppression endured by the Palestinians. In this era, the Palestinians formed a distinctive and undeniable collective identity that was deeply ingrained in their shared historical experiences, rich culture, and unwavering aspirations for self-governance. The burgeoning of this powerful nationalism fostered a profound sense of unity and propelled Palestinians beyond the confines of geographical and political disparities. The emergence of Palestinian national consciousness proved to be an invigorating force, permeating every realm of life and inspiring Palestinians from all walks of life to actively participate in the struggle to reclaim their rights and homeland. It became a potent driving force that galvanised the resistance efforts, sparking an impassioned dedication to the cause. This fervour laid a robust foundation for future generations, ensuring the perpetual continuity of the Palestinian struggle. The 1950s and 1960s marked a pivotal turning point in Palestinian history as the collective consciousness of the Palestinian people burgeoned and flourished, transcending the limitations imposed upon them. Palestinians solidified their identity by unifying their experiences, culture, and aspirations and coalesced into a formidable force. This collective identity, which blossomed amidst adversity, became the catalyst for resistance and provided a resilient framework for generations to come, ensuring that the Palestinian struggle would endure and prevail against all odds. (Abu Samra, 2020) (Haugbolle and Olsen, 2023).

5. 1970s: Intensification of Struggle

The 1970s witnessed a substantial intensification in the Palestinian fight against Zionist colonisation and subjugation. Palestinians firmly consolidated their resistance efforts to restore their inherent rights and cherished homeland. This epoch bore witness to many influential events that magnificently steered the direction of the struggle. From the renowned clash famously referred to as Black September, which served as a turning point, to the gripping conflict that ensued between the Jordanian government and various Palestinian factions, the 1970s became an indisputable milestone in history, etching itself as a profoundly significant chapter in the unwavering Palestinian pursuit of justice, liberation, and emancipation. Moreover, this period also witnessed the illustrious rise of determined armed groups, who valiantly took up the cause and garnered international attention, resulting in the resounding acknowledgement of the undeniable rights of the Palestinian people on a global scale. (Sabbagh-Khoury, 2023) (Khalidi, 2020).

5.1 BLACK SEPTEMBER AND JORDANIAN-PALESTINIAN CONFLICT

Among the pivotal episodes of the transformative and turbulent 1970s, the historic Black September conflict resonates profoundly. This fierce and momentous encounter unfolded as a relentless clash between Palestinian factions and the Jordanian government. Gripped by mounting apprehension caused by the escalating military power of the Palestinians within Jordan, the government staunchly initiated a swift and forceful military clampdown in September of 1970. The resultant confrontations, marred by sheer brutality and the ferocity of combat, unleashed a devastating wave of heavy casualties, sowing seeds of destruction and igniting unprecedented chaos. The ensuing cataclysm went far beyond physical strife as it unfurled into a cataclysmic cataclysm, triggering a massive and heart-wrenching large-scale displacement. Escaping the ravages of this bitter conflict, thousands of Palestinians were compelled to embark upon a poignant and painful search for sanctuary in the welcoming embrace of nearby countries, seeking solace and security in their dire moments of need. This epochal battle served to lay bare the deeply-rooted discord, animosity, and intransigence existing between the Jordanian government and Palestinian groups. With incendiary force, it exacerbated the inexorable and irreconcilable divergence that permeated their collective destinies. Amidst the scorching crucible of conflict, the struggle against Zionist subjugation resonated with an unwavering and defiant intensity, serving as a beacon of resilience, hope, and steadfast spirit for Palestinians determined to forge a path towards freedom, dignity, and self-determination. Undeterred by the adversities that beset them, the Palestinians emerged from this historic crucible strengthened, united, and more resolute than ever in their quest to shatter the chains of oppression and transcend the limits imposed upon them. Through their unwavering defiance and indomitable spirit, the Palestinians kindled flames of resistance that would reverberate across generations, inspiring countless others to stand tall against all forms of domination and injustice. In the annals of history, the Black September conflict occupies a hallowed place as a defining moment that indelibly heightens Palestinians' endurance, courage, and steadfastness in their unwavering pursuit of justice, dignity, and freedom. (Feldman, 2022) (Nijim, 2023) (Irfan, 2020) (Khalidi, 2020).

5.2 EMERGENCE OF PALESTINIAN ARMED GROUPS

Another significant progression that occurred during the 1970s was the emergence of Palestinian armed groups in response to the ongoing Zionist colonisation and occupation. Faced with repeated diplomatic setbacks and relentless aggression from Israel, the Palestinian people came to acknowledge the urgent need to exercise their rights and safeguard their land through armed conflict. Various organisations, including the Popular Front for the Liberation of Palestine (PFLP), the Democratic Front for the Liberation of Palestine (DFLP), and the Palestine Liberation Organisation (PLO), played vital roles in coordinating resistance operations, challenging the dominance of Zionist forces, and strengthening the Palestinian national identity. These groups became pivotal forces in the liberation struggle, offering a unified front against the oppressive occupation and working towards the restoration of Palestinian rights and self-determination. Their unwavering commitment to resistance demonstrated the resilience and determination of the Palestinian people in the face of immense challenges. It served as an assertion of their inherent right to exist and thrive on their ancestral land. (Barghouti, 2021) (Hroub2021).

5.3 INTERNATIONAL RECOGNITION OF PALESTINIAN RIGHTS

The 1970s also marked an important turning point in history concerning the increasing global acceptance and understanding of the Palestinian people's rightful claims and their struggle against Zionist colonisation and subjugation. The heroic resistance mounted by the Palestinians not only attracted attention but also garnered significant support from nations and international organisations all across the world. This overwhelming backing was a testament to the widespread recognition of the Palestinian cause, and it sent a clear message to the international community about the urgency of addressing the ongoing atrocities committed against the Palestinians. One of the most pivotal moments during this time was the endorsement of numerous resolutions by the United Nations, which unequivocally denounced the Israeli occupation and reaffirmed the inalienable rights of the Palestinian people. This show of international solidarity not only uplifted the spirits of the Palestinians but also exerted immense pressure on Israel to acknowledge and rectify the egregious wrongs that had been inflicted upon the Palestinian population for far too long. This crucial international recognition and support acted as a catalyst, igniting a spark that would fuel future diplomatic initiatives and global advocacy for Palestinian rights. It served as a rallying cry, galvanising individuals, governments, and organisations around the world to join forces and take a stand against the injustices faced by the Palestinians. This newfound momentum would ensure that the Palestinian cause would no longer be confined to the shadows but would instead be thrust into the spotlight, demanding immediate attention and action from the international community. It was a turning point that set the stage for a more inclusive and comprehensive discourse on Palestinian rights and a more determined pursuit of a just and lasting resolution to the Palestinian-Israeli conflict. (Imseis, 2020) (Barakat and Amouri, 2022) (Burba).

6. 1980s: Popular Uprising and International Solidarity

The 1980s was a tremendously important and transformative decade for the Palestinian struggle against the deeply entrenched and unjust system of Zionist settler-colonialism. During this time, a truly momentous event, known as the First Intifada, unfolded and forever altered the course of history. This grassroots rebellion, born out of a collective sense of frustration, suffering, and perpetual hardship under Israeli occupation, served as an inspiring and powerful response to the oppressive conditions endured by the Palestinian people. With a profound commitment to nonviolence, this courageous uprising employed diverse, peaceful tactics and strategies to challenge the occupying forces. The backbone of the First Intifada was formed by the sheer will and unwavering determination of ordinary Palestinians who courageously took to the streets, engaging in demonstrations marked by their sheer scale and ability to unite their people in a common cause. Thousands of Palestinians came together to voice their demands, aspirations, and unwavering belief in justice and freedom. In addition to the remarkable demonstrations, the First Intifada also witnessed numerous acts of civil resistance unfolding. Palestinians from all walks of life came together to orchestrate a vast array of activities aimed at undermining the structures of oppression imposed upon them by the Israeli authorities. From general strikes that brought entire cities and towns to a standstill to the boycotting of Israeli products, the Palestinians showcased their unyielding commitment to effecting change through peaceful means. The significance of the First Intifada reverberated far beyond the borders of Palestine, capturing the attention and garnering the international community's support. People from all corners of the globe, from all walks of life, stood in solidarity with the

Palestinian cause, recognising the urgency of the situation and the gravity of the injustices being perpetrated against the Palestinian people. Solidarity movements sprouted worldwide, vehemently condemning Israel's oppressive practices and advocating for the rights of the Palestinians. The global support generated by the First Intifada not only served as a source of hope for the Palestinians in their darkest hours but also played an instrumental role in exposing the true nature of Israel's occupation to the world. Through their collective efforts, the Palestinians were able to shed light on the profound injustices they endured daily, dismantle the fabricated narrative perpetuated by the Israeli authorities, and paint an accurate picture of the harsh realities faced by an entire population. The First Intifada was an extraordinary chapter in the ongoing struggle for justice and liberation. It symbolised the unwavering spirit, unity, and resilience of the Palestinian people while simultaneously challenging the oppressive status quo imposed upon them. The echoes of the First Intifada continue to reverberate through history, reminding us of the power inherent in collective action and the indomitable spirit of a people determined to reclaim their rights, dignity, and freedom. (Leopardi, 2020) (Gisle) (Leopardi and Leopardi2020) (Darweish2023).

6.1 FIRST INTIFADA: GRASSROOTS RESISTANCE MOVEMENT

Between 1987 and 1993, the First Intifada was a formidable grassroots resistance movement that emerged with great force, driven by the Palestinian public's immense determination and unwavering spirit. Deeply rooted in a seething discontent and a profound sense of injustice caused by Israeli occupation, the Intifada became a powerful symbol of resistance against oppressive authorities. The disgruntled Palestinians, refusing to accept the status quo, boldly challenged Israeli policies with unwavering resolve. They rose, defying the odds and embodying steadfast courage in adversity. The tactics employed during this historic resistance were carefully orchestrated, including the organisation of massive rallies that reverberated with the collective voice of the people. Additionally, widespread strikes paralysing the oppressive occupation machinery and acts of civil disobedience became powerful tools in dismantling the foundations of injustice. The First Intifada was an extraordinary display of unity and solidarity. Communities from all corners of Palestinian society joined together, recognising the urgency of their cause and forging an unbreakable bond. Through their relentless resistance, they sought to assert their inherent right to autonomy and to reclaim their stolen freedom. It was a remarkable testament to the power of grassroots movements, where ordinary individuals transcended their circumstances and became agents of change. Beyond the borders of Palestine, the First Intifada had a profound impact on a global scale. As news of the resistance spread far and wide, it ignited a spark of solidarity in people's hearts worldwide. The Palestinian struggle against Zionist occupation became a symbol of resistance against oppression and ignited a fervour within the international community. The First Intifada served as a wake-up call, awakening a dormant awareness and galvanising support for the righteous Palestinian cause.

In both its power and persistence, the First Intifada emerged as a defining moment in the history of Palestinian resistance. It showcased the indomitable spirit of a people yearning for justice and freedom, willing to defy all odds and risk everything for their inherent rights. Through their unwavering determination, Palestinians fought for their liberation. They became beacons of hope for oppressed peoples worldwide, proving that collective action and unwavering resolve can spark meaningful change in the face of oppression. (Naser-Najjab, 2020) (Leopardi, 2020) (Jabali, 2022).

6.2 ROLE OF WOMEN IN THE PALESTINIAN STRUGGLE

Throughout the illustrious and storied years of unwavering Palestinian resistance against the formidable forces of Zionist oppression, the resolute and indomitable presence of women has undeniably emerged as a beacon of inspiration and a formidable force in the fight for liberation. Navigating through the treacherous labyrinth of multidimensional subjugation, Palestinian women have showcased remarkable resilience, unwavering commitment, and unfaltering courage as impassioned activists on the frontlines of change. Their steadfast dedication and unyielding spirit transpire into diverse forms of resistance, spanning from grassroots mobilisation that pulsates through the very core of Palestinian society to assuming pivotal roles in political leadership, thereby influencing the trajectory of the Palestinian struggle at its very foundation. Embodying the essence of empowerment, Palestinian women have ceaselessly organised and spearheaded protests, their collective voices reverberating through the soundwaves of dissent, as they valiantly confront the oppressive forces that seek to suppress their inalienable rights. Fearlessly embracing the flames of resistance, they stand shoulder to shoulder with their comrades, valiantly engaging in combative confrontations with unwavering strength and a ferocious determination to dismantle the shackles of injustice. Yet, their noble contributions extend far beyond the borders of their homeland, as Palestinian women tirelessly advocate for the rights of their people on the global stage, commanding attention and compelling action from the international community. Catalysing change and raising global awareness, their unwavering advocacy serves as an unyielding testament to the power of unity, solidarity, and the steadfast pursuit of justice. Indeed, their participation in the struggle against the oppressive societal norms that seek to subjugate Palestinian women reinforces the resilient fabric of Palestinian society. By challenging systemic inequalities and defying the limits imposed upon them, Palestinian women demonstrate the unwavering spirit and boundless potential within their collective consciousness, igniting a transformative ripple effect that resonates far beyond their immediate circumstances. (Zichi, 2021) (Abdo, 2021)As the influence of Palestinian women within the multifaceted struggle for liberation continues to evolve and expand, their unwavering commitment and unwavering tenacity serve as a beacon of hope, inspiring future generations to rise and seize their rightful place in the fight for freedom, justice, and equality. Their relentless pursuit of a brighter future, infused with the unyielding spirit of Palestinian resistance, reverberates through the annals of history, leaving an indelible mark on the world and instilling a flame of hope that burns eternally within the hearts and minds of all those who dare to dream of a world unbound by the chains of oppression. (Gandhi, 2022).

6.3 GLOBAL SUPPORT FOR THE PALESTINIAN CAUSE

The Palestinian cause has garnered immense and overwhelming support on a global scale, with people from all walks of life and all corners of the world standing in solidarity against the oppressive forces of Zionist colonialism and the unwarranted persecution faced by the Palestinian people. This unwavering support is evident through many actions and initiatives, spanning from tireless activism aimed at shedding light on the Palestinian plight to the provision of much-needed humanitarian aid and the implementation of vital policy measures and diplomatic interventions. It is heartening to witness the immense dedication and commitment displayed by civil society institutions, human rights organisations, and countless individuals who tirelessly advocate for Palestinian rights. Through their unwavering efforts, they strive to raise awareness about the injustices faced by the Palestinian people and shed light on the grave violations of their basic human rights. These champions of justice play a pivotal role in amplifying the voices of the oppressed, ensuring that the world hears their stories and understands their struggles. Moreover, numerous nations around the globe staunchly align themselves with the Palestinian cause, unequivocally endorsing the urgent need for an end to the illegal occupation and the establishment of a fully autonomous Palestinian state. These countries join forces to bring international attention to the plight of the Palestinian people, both in their capacities and through cooperative efforts. Their united front is a powerful testament to the global consensus on the importance of human rights, justice, and the right to self-determination (Hroub2021) (Barghouti, 2021). The resounding and unwavering support for the Palestinian cause serves as a reminder of the collective moral compass of humanity but also reaffirms the universal acceptance of human rights principles. It underscores that the fight for justice and liberty, transcending geographical borders and cultural differences, knows no boundaries. This global backing for the Palestinian people reiterates the fundamental belief in the inherent dignity and worth of every individual, irrespective of their ethnic, religious, or national background. Thus, as we continue to pursue justice, equality, and dignity for all, let us take inspiration from the steadfast support for the Palestinian cause. Let us draw strength from the unity displayed by individuals, organisations, and nations worldwide as we work collectively towards a future where every individual can exercise their basic human rights, free from the shackles of oppression and persecution. Together, we can build a world where justice is not merely a distant ideal but a lived reality for each of us. (Khalidi, 2020) (Barghouti, 2021) (Sexton2023).

7. 1990s: Oslo Accords and Fragmentation

During the decade of the 1990s, a significant landmark was realised in the form of the historic Oslo Accords, which marked a milestone in the ongoing Israeli-Palestinian dispute. These groundbreaking accords sought to meticulously outline and address the complex contours of the conflict, with both the Palestine Liberation Organisation (PLO) and Israel appending their signatures to these transformative agreements. The primary objective was to pave the way for a peaceful settlement and foster a conducive environment for Palestinians to exercise self-governance in the territories that had been invaded. However, despite the initial hope and optimism surrounding the Oslo Accords, their implementation yielded unexpected consequences that deeply impacted the Palestinians. Rather than fostering enduring tranquillity and solidarity, these accords inadvertently led to the fragmentation and division of Palestinian society. The partitioning of the West Bank and Gaza Strip, accompanied by the establishment of the Palestinian Authority, created a sense of disruption and disunity, eroding the cohesive national fabric and undermining the collective resistance against Zionist colonialism and subjugation. The Oslo Accords, while representing a significant step forward in terms of diplomatic engagement and negotiation, did not manage to fulfil their intended objectives. Instead, they highlighted the complexities and multifaceted nature of the Israeli-Palestinian conflict, revealing the intricate dynamics at play and the challenge of finding a just and lasting resolution. The period following the accords demonstrated the need for sustained dialogue, inclusive negotiations, and a comprehensive approach that addresses both sides' legitimate aspirations and concerns. Only through such deeply engaged and open discussions can a framework for a truly peaceful coexistence that respects the rights, dignity, and self-determination of all parties involved be established. (Jaber, 2020) (Morrison, 2020) (Nasasra, 2021).

7.1 OSLO PEACE PROCESS AND ITS IMPLICATIONS

Launched in the 1990s, the Oslo Peace Process significantly impacted the Palestinian movement towards independence. It created a framework for discussions between the Palestine Liberation Organisation (PLO) and the government of Israel, intending to institute a two-state solution that would ensure lasting peace in the region. Nonetheless, the process fell short of addressing the fundamental triggers of the dispute, including the return rights of Palestinian refugees and the matter of Israeli settlements, which continue to be a major point of contention between the two sides. Furthermore, the Oslo Peace Process inadvertently catalysed the formation of the Palestinian Authority. This governing body was intended to serve as the go-between between the Israeli occupation and the Palestinian society. However, instead of alleviating tensions and promoting progress towards statehood, it unintentionally deepened the prevalent power disequilibrium and undermined the visions of Palestinian self-determination and sovereign statehood. As a result, while initially hailed as a significant step towards peace and stability in the region, the

Oslo Peace Process ultimately failed to achieve its intended objectives. It highlighted the pressing need for comprehensive negotiations that address core issues, such as the right of return for Palestinian refugees and the status of Israeli settlements, to foster genuine reconciliation and pave the way for a just and lasting resolution to the Israeli-Palestinian conflict. Despite its shortcomings, the Oslo Peace Process was an important starting point for future diplomatic efforts and laid the groundwork for subsequent negotiations. It demonstrated the potential for dialogue and cooperation between the two parties, even in deep-rooted divisions and distrust. It also brought international attention to the Israeli-Palestinian conflict and reaffirmed the international community's commitment to finding a peaceful resolution. Moving forward, building upon the lessons learnt from the Oslo Peace Process and working towards a more inclusive and comprehensive approach to peacebuilding is imperative. This includes acknowledging the rights and aspirations of both the Israeli and Palestinian people while addressing the underlying causes of the conflict and ensuring equal participation and representation for all parties involved. Ultimately, the path to lasting peace and stability in the Israeli-Palestinian conflict lies in sincere and meaningful negotiations that address the core issues at hand. Only through a genuine commitment to dialogue, mutual respect, and compromise can the aspirations of both Israelis and Palestinians for a secure and prosperous future be truly realised. (Morrison, 2020) (Enderlin, 2021) (Atallah, 2021).

7.2 RISE OF HAMAS AND ISLAMIC RESISTANCE

The ineffective fulfilment of the Oslo Accords in enhancing the Palestinians' lives prepared the ground for the emergence of Hamas and Islamic resistance movements in the 1990s. The peace process's stagnancy and failure to deliver on its promises drove numerous Palestinians towards these factions as alternative bulwarks against Zionist colonialism and subjugation, thereby seeking a more effective means of resistance and liberation. Hamas, particularly, not only garnered a significant following but also emerged as a formidable political powerhouse, fuelled by its unwavering dedication to armed struggle and the establishment of an Islamic state within the historical confines of Palestine. This ascendance of Hamas, accompanied by the rise of other Islamic resistance factions, presented a substantial challenge to the previously dominant secular Palestine Liberation Organisation (PLO), thereby further complicating the already intricate and intricate political landscape of Palestine. The complex interplay between these factions and alliances, each with its own ideological underpinnings and strategic objectives, led to an even greater fragmentation of Palestinian politics, resulting in an intricate web of competing interests and aspirations that demanded astute navigational skills and diplomacy to unravel. Consequently, the evolving political landscape of Palestine witnessed unprecedented diversity and complexity, underscoring the need for a comprehensive and inclusive approach to address the multifaceted challenges facing the Palestinian people. The emergence of Hamas and other Islamic resistance movements in response to the shortcomings of the Oslo Accords not only altered the dynamics of the Israeli-Palestinian conflict but also demonstrated the resilience and determination of the Palestinian people in their pursuit of self-determination and liberation. Furthermore, the growing influence of these factions highlighted the limitations of the traditional, secular framework in addressing the aspirations and grievances of the Palestinian population, necessitating a more nuanced and inclusive approach that takes into account the multifaceted nature of Palestinian society. As the political landscape continued to evolve and adapt, the presence of Hamas and other Islamic resistance movements served as a stark reminder of the complexities inherent in the pursuit of peace, justice, and freedom in the region. Therefore, it became increasingly clear that any comprehensive resolution to the Israeli-Palestinian conflict must encompass not only political considerations but also cultural, religious, and socio-economic dimensions in order to achieve a sustainable and just peace for all parties involved. (Alsoos, 2021) (Awad, 2021) (Tamimi) (Hamed, 2021).

7.3 SETTLER EXPANSION AND LAND CONFISCATION

The decade of the 1990s bore witness to a deeply concerning and unsettling surge in settler expansion and seizure of land in the occupied Palestinian territories. During this period, the Israeli settlements, which were widely regarded as illicit under international legal parameters, experienced exponential growth and proliferation. This rapid expansion was primarily fuelled by the endorsement and support of the Israeli authorities, who encouraged and facilitated the influx of Jewish settlers into the West Bank and Gaza Strip. As the settlements multiplied, the consequences became increasingly dire for the Palestinian people. Not only did the annexation of Palestinian lands occur, but the incremental fragmentation of Palestinian territories also took place. This relentless process made the realisation of a viable and independent state of Palestine seemingly unattainable as the land continued to be aggressively encroached upon by Israeli settlers. Adding to the complex situation, the Israeli military presence often served as protection for the settlements, exacerbating the hardships faced by Palestinian communities. The proliferation of settlements resulted in the dispersal of Palestinian populations, further contributing to the loss of vital sources of income and exacerbating socio-economic challenges for the native population. Consequently, the cycle of Zionist colonialism and domination persisted and intensified, perpetuating a systematic imbalance of power and control in the region. (Keelan and Browne, 2020) (Hallaq2020).

8. 2000s: Second Intifada and Changing Dynamics

The onset of the 21st century ushered in a seminal era in Palestinian resistance - the epoch of the Second Intifada. This pivotal period, characterised by intense frustration and indignation, arose as a direct result of the fruitless attempts at peace negotiations and the ceaseless Israeli occupation that plagued the Palestinian people. The growing discontentment among Palestinians culminated in a wave of far-reaching protests, expansive public demonstrations, and a surge in resistance activities. The epoch was unequivocally defined by a notable shift in the resistance paradigm, as Palestinians increasingly embraced the notions of armed resistance and urban guerrilla tactics. It was through the Second Intifada that the Palestinians wholeheartedly and resolutely articulated their deep-seated grievances and unyielding determination to defy and oppose the oppressive forces of Zionist imperialism and relentless repression. Consequently, the Second Intifada served as an unprecedented catalyst for the mobilisation of Palestinian civil society, sparking an outpouring of courageous resistance against the occupation forces. The widespread participation of Palestinians from all walks of life, including students, workers, professionals, and grassroots activists, emboldened the movement and magnified their collective voices. This empowered sense of unity and solidarity among Palestinians was aptly demonstrated through widespread acts of civil disobedience, which included strikes, boycotts, and mass mobilisations. Israeli military checkpoints and settlements became focal points of resistance, with Palestinians organising sit-ins, demonstrations, and creative forms of nonviolent resistance to challenge the occupiers. Moreover, the Second Intifada revitalised the role of women in the resistance movement, as they emerged as prominent leaders and key contributors to the struggle for freedom and justice. Women's involvement in various spheres of resistance, such as organising protests, providing medical aid, and disseminating information, underscored their unwavering commitment to the cause. Despite the brutal tactics employed by the Israeli military and security forces to suppress the resistance, including targeted assassinations, mass arrests, and punitive measures, the Palestinians persevered and defied all odds. The Second Intifada was a powerful testament to the resilience and determination of the Palestinian people, who continued to resist and seek their rightful self-determination. By highlighting the inhumane conditions endured under the oppressive occupation, the Second Intifada drew global attention and support for the Palestinian cause, fuelling a renewed international awareness and solidarity. It further underscored the urgent need for a just and lasting solution that respects the rights and aspirations of the Palestinian people. Thus, the Second Intifada is a poignant chapter in the ongoing struggle for freedom, justice, and the realisation of Palestinian rights. (Brunner and Amrami, 2021) (Hawari, 2021) (Sahhar2023).

8.1 FAILURE OF PEACE NEGOTIATIONS

In spite of the plethora of myriad peace conciliation rounds that transpired in the 21st century, comprising the historical 2000 Camp David Summit and the highly anticipated 2007 Annapolis Conference, the pervasive hope for an equitable and enduring peace between Israelis and Palestinians remained regrettably unfulfilled. The unfortunate breakdown of these arduous negotiations stemmed from a multitude of causes, ranging from the glaring disparity in negotiation strength between the two parties to the ceaseless and controversial expansion of Israeli settlements on Palestinian lands, all the while grappling with the deeply complex and unresolved principal matters such as borders, Jerusalem's disputed status, and the oft-thorny right of return for Palestinian refugees. The devastating collapse of these painstaking negotiation efforts not only exacerbated the already palpable Palestinian resistance but also ignited a renewed and rekindled sense of indomitable commitment amongst Palestinians to relentlessly strive for justice, self-determination, and the long-awaited realisation of their legitimate aspirations. (Ben-Ami, 2022) (Dekel and Moran-Gilad, 2021) (Kurtzer, 2020).

8.2 ISRAELI MILITARY OPERATIONS AND HUMAN RIGHTS VIOLATIONS

The turn of the millennium, a pivotal moment in history, witnessed a series of bold and far-reaching Israeli military operations within the occupied Palestinian territories. These operations, reaching their apex with the profound intensity of Operation Defencive Shield in 2002 and Operation Cast Lead spanning from 2008 to 2009, left an indelible mark on the collective consciousness of both Palestinians and the world. They were characterised by the relentless and expansive incursions of Israeli forces, the relentless aerial bombardments of Palestinian territories, and the ruthless deployment of formidable weaponry upon the unsuspecting Palestinian civilian population. Tragically, these acts of aggression perpetrated by the Israeli military unleashed an unprecedented torrent of suffering and despair. Palestinian lives were tragically lost, their inherent right to existence violently torn asunder. The very fabric of their homes and essential infrastructure was mercilessly obliterated, leaving a harrowing trail of destruction in its wake. The waves of displacement that ensued unleashed heartache and upheaval upon several thousand Palestinians, forever altering the course of their lives. The international community, burdened by the weight of witnessing such immense devastation and deplorable disregard for human rights, resoundingly condemned these acts of violence. The disproportional use of force employed by the Israeli military casts a glaring light upon the transgressions against the principles cherished by humanity. The world, unified in its disdain, rallied behind the call for resistance against the insidious spectre of Zionist colonisation, recognising the urgent need to safeguard the intrinsic rights and dignity of the Palestinian people. (Nijim, 2020) (Raby, 2023) (Loewenstein, 2023).

8.3 INTERNATIONAL BOYCOTT, DIVESTMENT, AND SANCTIONS MOVEMENT

In reaction to the numerous violations of human rights committed by the Israeli occupation, the international community witnessed the unmistakable emergence and growth of the Boycott, Divestment, and Sanctions (BDS) movement during the 2000s. Rooted in the fundamental principle of nonviolence, the BDS movement sought to exert significant pressure on Israel, compelling it to adhere to international legal standards and recognise the inherent rights of the Palestinian people. To achieve this noble objective, the BDS movement advocated for a comprehensive boycott of goods produced within Israeli territories, as well as corporations that profited from the ongoing occupation. Furthermore, it called for divestment from Israeli firms and the imposition of internationally-backed sanctions against the Israeli administration. Within an impressively short span of time, the BDS movement gained remarkable traction on a global scale, garnering the support and endorsement of numerous esteemed academic institutions, influential businesses, and notable personalities. Its profound impact was felt far and wide, serving as a potent instrument of international solidarity for the Palestinian cause. Consequently, it wielded immense pressure on Israel, compelling the nation to reconsider and ultimately discontinue its oppressive policies. Through steadfast determination and unwavering commitment, the BDS movement succeeded in amplifying the voices of the oppressed and heralding a new era of justice, equality, and respect for human rights in the Israeli-Palestinian conflict. (Lustick and Shils, 2022) (Baig, 2022).

9. 2010s: Resilience and Resurgence

The decade of 2010-2020 bore witness to a remarkably persistent Palestinian resistance movement, even in the face of relentless colonisation and suppression. Palestinians held their ground, demanding righteousness and fairness, steadfastly determined to overcome the obstacles that stood in their way. This decade was illuminated by a rekindled dedication towards their liberation, employing many resistance modalities as diverse as they were powerful. Ranging from stirring artistic and cultural expressions that captivated the world's attention to peaceful protests that echoed with unwavering conviction, the Palestinians harnessed the strength of their collective voice to push for change. They also engaged in legal altercations, skillfully navigating the complex legal systems that sought to undermine their cause. In the face of immense adversity, the Palestinians manifested their resilience, refusing to succumb to despair or hopelessness. They emerged as an indomitable force, their unwavering spirit shining brightly in the 2010s, symbolising the Palestinian population's unyielding resolve. From every corner of their homeland, they stood together, unflinchingly refusing to be stifled and perpetually combating for their basic human rights, dignity, and sovereignty. In this decade of unwavering struggle, the Palestinians exemplified the strength and determination within the human spirit, reminding us of the power of resilience and the importance of standing up for what is right. (Darweish2023) (Alakhras and Ariffin..., 2022) (Saleh, 2022).

9.1 PALESTINIAN CULTURAL AND ARTISTIC RESISTANCE

Historically, Palestinians have not only embraced but also leveraged their rich culture and art as potent and formidable instruments for combating and challenging Zionist colonisation and subjugation. Throughout the 2010s, the Palestinian artistic and cultural resistance movement experienced a remarkable blossoming, emerging as a method to safeguard their deeply rooted traditions, contest dominant narratives, and assert their group identity. With diverse artistic expressions such as music, literature, movies, visual arts, and more, the Palestinians have fearlessly wielded their creative talents to showcase their abundant cultural heritage and convey their deep-seated torments and resolute hopes. In these endeavours, the untiring efforts of artists and cultural establishments have borne a pivotal role, tirelessly fostering international consciousness and forging meaningful shared experiences among Palestinians, uniting them in their collective act of resistance. (Slitine, 2022) (Corm, 2020)This powerful and transformative form of resistance, which has taken root in culture and art, has grown into a profound source of dignity and resilience for Palestinians. It has undoubtedly established an invaluable platform for magnifying their voices, enabling them to powerfully and unapologetically narrate their tales. Through these artistic expressions, the intrepid Palestinians have seized agency over their narratives and reclaimed their rightful place in history, defying attempts at erasure and elevating their struggle to the forefront of global awareness. Thus, the artistic and cultural resistance of the Palestinians stands tall as a testament to their unwavering spirit, unyielding resilience, and unbreakable bond with their cultural heritage. It serves as a resounding reminder that their art becomes a weapon in the face of adversity, their creativity a force, and their collective resistance a beacon of hope for a better future. (Dae Cesari, 2021) (Boren, 2022).

9.2 GREAT MARCH OF RETURN AND NONVIOLENT RESISTANCE

The 2010s saw the Great March of Return - a series of peaceful protests initiated by Palestinians in the Gaza Strip - as one of the most notable acts of resistance in recent history. Kicked off in 2018, Palestinians, including children, women, and men from all walks of life, united in their determination and took to the streets to stage peaceful demonstrations along the Israeli border, advocating for the right of return for Palestinian refugees and expressing their dissent against the unjust Israeli barricade that restricted their freedom and rights. Despite the tremendous challenges and the unimaginable violence unleashed upon them by Israeli troops, the Palestinian demonstrators showcased unwavering bravery and steadfastness in their commitment to nonviolent resistance. Their courageous defiance not only inspired those around them but also captivated the international community's attention, sparking a global conversation and reshaping the narrative surrounding the deeply rooted Palestinian conflict. The Great March of Return served as undeniable proof of the effectiveness of peaceful resistance in dismantling oppressive and inequitable systems. By standing up against injustice and advocating for their rights, the Palestinians in the Gaza Strip shed light on the longstanding injustices and human rights violations perpetrated under the Israeli occupation. Their peaceful protests demonstrated the power of collective action and the strength of the human spirit, leaving an indelible mark on the annals of history and inspiring generations to come. (Jones, 2023) (Pace aet al., 2021) (Stefanini, 2021).

9.3 LEGAL CHALLENGES TO ISRAELI OCCUPATION

During the transformative and tumultuous decade of the 2010s, Palestinians and their valiant allies embarked upon an unprecedented journey that yielded remarkable and momentous accomplishments in their noble quest to challenge and confront the flagrant Israeli occupation through the formidable power of legal recourse. With admirable resolve and unwavering determination, they deftly harnessed the robust and indispensable frameworks of international law to exact a long-overdue semblance of justice and hold the occupier, Israel, rigorously accountable for its manifold transgressions against the inalienable rights of the Palestinian people and the insidious proliferation of illegal settlements that continue to undermine the very foundations of peace in the region. Amidst this ardent pursuit of truth and justice, Palestinian legal experts, bolstered ceaselessly by the solidarity of prominent human rights organisations, embarked upon an indomitable crusade, meticulously documenting and forcefully exposing the manifold depredations committed by Israel. Motivated by an unwavering commitment to the cause of justice and empathy for the victims, these unwavering champions left no stone unturned in their relentless quest to secure fairness for the oppressed and demand unequivocal accountability for the oppressor. Without any hesitation, these legal luminaries intensified their efforts by initiating a wide array of legal actions in both the domestic and international tribunals, strategically targeting the highest echelons of the Israeli government, as well as the insidious corporations that knowingly and wilfully contribute to perpetuating the occupation. These bold legal challenges, designed with the utmost precision, not only encompassed the grave violations committed by Israeli officials but also harnessed the power of the law to protect and preserve the sacred rights of the Palestinian people to their ancestral land, their cherished access to water resources, and the unassailable right to self-rule. It is through these audacious and tenacious excursions along the corridors of justice that the flame of hope was rekindled within the hearts of a beleaguered population, yearning for a genuine and lasting resolution to the relentless affront that they have borne with stoicism and unwavering fortitude. Pursuing justice through legal avenues provided a glimmer of optimism, breathing new life into the struggle for freedom, dignity, and sovereignty that courses through the Palestinian people's collective aspirations and indomitable spirit. (Jones, 2023) (Pace aet al., 2021) (Stefanini, 2021) (Harrold2020) (El Kurd, 2022).

10. Future Prospects: Challenges and Hope

Facing forward, the Palestinian fight against Zionist subjugation and colonialism not only brings forth numerous trials but also sparks a glimmering sense of optimism when contemplating prospects. The persistent territorial control, land annexation, and ruthless colonisation orchestrated by settlers present significant hurdles in the Palestinian quest for autonomy and self-rule. The policies perpetuated by the Israeli government consistently sow discontentment and desolation among the Palestinian population, igniting an even more formidable surge of resistance within their hearts. Nevertheless, amidst these seemingly insurmountable adversities, a small yet resilient beacon of hope remains alight. The unwavering spirit of the Palestinian people, characterised by their tenacity and fortitude in the face of overwhelming odds, is fortified by escalating global empathy and growing cognisance regarding their immense tribulations. Through this compassion and understanding, the potential for a brighter and more prosperous future for Palestine begins to emerge. Though uncertain, these future prospects hang delicately in the balance of the global community's unwavering resolve to uphold principles of justice, human rights, and international laws. By lending a louder and more resolute voice to the Palestinian crusade and tangibly supporting their cause, there is the possibility of constructing a fairer, more equitable, and harmonious future for Palestine and its people. It is through collective efforts and solidarity that the foundations of a just and lasting peace can be truly established, ensuring the Palestinian population's rightful place in the global community. As the international community continues to heighten its awareness and understanding of the Palestinian struggle, there is an increasing potential for meaningful change and progress. Together, let us stand united, decrying the injustices inflicted upon the Palestinian people and advocating for their right to self-determination and freedom. Through our collective actions and unwavering support, we can move closer to the realisation of a future in which Palestine thrives, its people flourish, and coexistence prevails. Now is the time to act and forge a path towards a better world, one where the hopes and dreams of the Palestinian people can finally take root and blossom into a reality. (Finkelstein, 2021) (Stefanini, 2021) (Harrold2020).

10.1 IMPACTS OF ANNEXATION AND SETTLER COLONIALISM

The far-reaching and profound implications of the contentious issue surrounding land annexation and colonisation by settlers on Palestinian resistance movements cannot be underestimated. Historically, the policies adopted in favour of annexation and the relentless encroachment of illegal Israeli settlements have had devastating consequences for the Palestinian people. These actions have led to the brazen seizure of Palestinian lands, resulting in the forcible uprooting and displacement of entire communities, and, in turn, have caused the fragmentation and splintering of the Palestinian territory. Such actions not only pose significant challenges to the tireless efforts of Palestinians to achieve their long-desired independence but also serve to intensify and fortify the very occupation they seek to challenge. One of the most enduring and engendering factors that inevitably engenders tensions between Israelis and Palestinians lies in the steadfast and unwavering presence of Israeli settlers in the West Bank and East Jerusalem. This continued inhabitation is a constant reminder of the disputed nature of the territories, igniting an ever-present and volatile source of conflict. The clash of opposing ideologies, interests, and aspirations fuels a never-ending cycle of resistance, breeds aggression and further deepens the divide. To reach a harmonious and equitable settlement, it is of paramount importance to not only acknowledge but also to actively counteract the detrimental and cascading effects of annexation and settler colonialism. By doing so, it becomes possible to chart a course towards a just and permanent resolution to the longstanding Israeli-Palestinian conflict. Only through concerted efforts to address the immense challenges posed by these systemic issues can a comprehensive and sustainable solution be achieved, one that paves the way for a future of coexistence, peace, and prosperity for all parties involved. (Nijim, 2020) (Schleifer, 2022) (Nijim, 2023).

10.2 ROLE OF INTERNATIONAL COMMUNITY IN RESOLVING THE CONFLICT

The International community plays an incredibly significant role in addressing and resolving the complex Israeli-Palestinian strife that has ravaged the region for decades. Due to the relentless Palestinian resistance against Zionist subjugation and colonisation, it is imperative for the global community to extend its outreach and actively engage in finding a fair and just resolution. In order to achieve this, it is crucial for the international community to effectively utilise diplomatic means to exert pressure on Israel, compelling them to abide by international laws, put an end to the occupation, and fully recognise the legitimate rights of the Palestinian people. In addition to these measures, it is essential for the international community to provide unwavering support to grassroots movements that are working tirelessly to bring about positive change. By advocating for accountability in cases of human rights infringements, the global community can ensure that those responsible for such violations are held responsible for their actions. Moreover, fostering open and constructive discussions, as well as facilitating negotiations, are paramount steps on the path to achieving lasting peace and justice in the region. It is of utmost importance that the international community demonstrates its unwavering commitment towards an equitable resolution, as it serves as a critical safeguard for the rights of the Palestinian people and the establishment of a sustainable and independent Palestinian nation. Only through a collective effort can we hope to bring an end to the conflicts and pave the way for a brighter future for all those involved. The time for action and solidarity is now. (Nijim, 2023) (Uddin, 2022).

10.3 PALESTINIAN YOUTH AND THE CONTINUATION OF RESISTANCE

Palestinian youth are instrumental in prolonging the resistance against Zionist subjugation and colonialism. Despite being raised under the oppression of occupation, they have emerged as influential agents of transformation, epitomising unparalleled resilience, unwavering valour, and indomitable determination. This vibrant and empowered younger generation spearheads an array of grassroots initiatives, fearlessly voicing their relentless pursuit of justice, liberation, and equality. Through their profound expressions in various mediums such as art, music, online activism, and active community engagement, Palestinian youth intensify their voices while simultaneously fostering a heightened global consciousness surrounding their valiant struggle. Their supremely unwavering tenacity in upholding their inalienable rights and unquenchable desire for self-rule resounds magnificently, echoing the resounding power of the Palestinian resistance. We must instil unwavering confidence and provide steadfast support to the Palestinian youth, for it is through their invincible spirit that the resistance movement shall flourish, ensuring its longevity and ultimate triumph. The young Palestinian generation, in their unwavering commitment towards combating Zionist subjugation and colonialism, plays a critical role in advancing the resistance. Despite coming of age in a state of occupation, they have emerged as an influential force driving transformation and embodying an extraordinary level of resilience, steadfast courage, and unwavering determination. This dynamic and empowered youth cohort leads a myriad of grassroots initiatives fearlessly, asserting their unwavering pursuit of justice, liberation, and equality. Their profound expressions through diverse mediums, including art, music, online activism, and active community participation, serve to amplify their voices and raise global awareness about their noble struggle. The sheer strength of their unyielding resolve in upholding their inherent rights and tireless quest for self-determination resonates with splendour, echoing the resounding power of the Palestinian resistance. We must nurture their unwavering confidence and offer steadfast support to the Palestinian youth, as it is through their invincible spirit, the resistance movement will thrive, ensuring its enduring existence and ultimate triumph. (Nijim, 2020) (Finkelstein, 2021) (Pace aet al., 2021).

References:

Reinharz, J. and Golani, M. "Chaim Weizmann: The great enabler. From the Balfour Declaration to the establishment of the state of Israel." Modern Judaism (2020).HTML

Loevy, Karin. "The Balfour Declaration's Territorial Landscape: Between Protection and Self-Determination." Humanity: An International Journal of Human Rights, Humanitarianism, and Development 12, no. 2 (2021): 138-158.HTML

Khalidi, R. "The hundred years' war on Palestine: A history of settler colonialism and resistance, 1917–2017." (2020).HTML

Abukmeil, T. N. S. "Popular resistance in Palestine as a national action strategy." (2022).izu.edu.tr

Dana, T. "Localising the Economy as a Resistance Response: A Contribution to the "Resistance Economy" Debate in the Occupied Palestinian Territories." Journal of Peacebuilding & Development (2020).HTML

Kayali, L. "Palestinian Women and Popular Resistance: Perceptions, Attitudes, and Strategies." (2020).HTML

Hurewitz, J. C. "The struggle for Palestine." (2022).HTML

Alqaisiya, W. "Beyond the contours of Zionist sovereignty: Decolonisation in Palestine's Unity Intifada." Political Geography (2023).lse.ac.uk

Cohen, M. J. "The British Mandate in Palestine: A Centenary Volume, 1920–2020." (2020).HTML

Hyamson, A. M. "Palestine under the mandate: 1920-1948." (2022).HTML

Cohen, M. J. "The British Mandate in Palestine." api.taylorfrancis.com .HTML

Manna, A. "Nakba and Survival: The Story of Palestinians Who Remained in Haifa and the Galilee, 1948–1956." (2022).oapen.org

Juliana, A. "Forced Migration: The 1948 Palestinian Refugees." Hadtudományi Szemle (2023).ludovika.hu

Saadah, M. J. "The Palestinian Perspective: Understanding the Legacy of al-Nakba Through the Palestinian Narrative." Berkeley Undergraduate Journal (2021).escholarship.org

Imseis, A. "The United Nations plan of partition for Palestine revisited: On the origins of Palestine's international legal subalternity." Stan. J. Int'l L. (2021).HTML

Pressman, J. "History in conflict: Israeli–Palestinian speeches at the United Nations, 1998–2016." Mediterranean Politics (2020).HTML

Barakat, M. and Amouri, Y. "Who is representing the Palestinian People: The Palestine Liberation Organization or the State of Palestine? The Aftermath of United Nations General Assembly …." Arab Law Quarterly (2022).HTML

Irfan, A. "Palestine at the UN: The PLO and UNRWA in the 1970s." Journal of Palestine Studies (2020).ucl.ac.uk

Darraj, O. "The relationship between the PLO and the Palestinian National Authority." (2020).HTML

Barak, O., Sheniak, A., and Shapira, A. "The shift to

defence in Israel's hybrid military strategy." Journal of Strategic Studies (2023).academia.edu

Hamdan, H. "The Role of Palestinian Resistance in Maintaining the Conflict Status Quo." (2023).aub.edu.lb

Samra, Mjriam Abu, and Loubna Qutami. "Alterity Across Generations. A Comparative Analysis of the 1950's Jeel al-Thawra and the 2006 Palestinian Youth Movement." Revue des mondes musulmans et de la Méditerranée 147 (2020).openedition.org

Kimmerling, B. "Politicide: Ariel Sharon's war against the Palestinians." (2020).HTML

Khan, H. "Seeking Solidarity: The Emergence of a Black-American Connection with Palestine, 1890s-1970s." (2022).unc.edu

Dalal, A. "The refugee camp as urban housing." Housing Studies (2022).sfb1265.de

Plakans, A. "Resettlement Years: The 1950s." The Reluctant Exiles (2021).HTML

Fitili, Magda, Virgiliu Țârău, Dzeneta Karabegović, Massoud Sharifi, Merlys Mosquera, Rolland Fosso, Paul Mulholland, Marc Hernández, and Mikel Zorrilla. "From So Far to So Close. Addressing the Refugee Phenomenon: History, Sociology, Technology." In International Conference: From So Far to So Close. Addressing the Refugee Phenomenon: History, Sociology and Technology (June 15-16th, Virtual Format). 2020.uab.cat

Abu Samra, M. "The Palestinian transnational student movement 1948-1982: a study on popular organization and transnational mobilization." (2020).ox.ac.uk

Haugbolle, S. and Olsen, P. V. "Emergence of Palestine

as a Global Cause." Middle East Critique (2023).tandfonline.com

Sabbagh-Khoury, A. "Colonizing Palestine: The Zionist Left and the Making of the Palestinian Nakba." (2023).HTML

Khalidi, R. "The hundred years' war on Palestine: A history of settler colonialism and resistance, 1917–2017." (2020).HTML

Feldman, I. "Conflicted presence: The many arrivals of Palestinians in Lebanon." Migration Studies (2022).oup.com

Nijim, M. "Genocide in Palestine: Gaza as a case study." The International Journal of Human Rights (2023).HTML

Khalidi, R. "The hundred years' war on Palestine: A history of settler colonialism and resistance, 1917–2017." (2020).HTML

Barghouti, O. "BDS: Nonviolent, globalized Palestinian resistance to Israel's settler colonialism and apartheid." Journal of Palestine Studies (2021).HTML

Hroub, Khaled. "Palestinian Nationalism, Religious (Un) claims, and the Struggle against Zionism." When Politics Are Sacralized: Comparative Perspectives on Religious Claims and Nationalism (2021): 365.ashoka.edu.in

Imseis, A. "Negotiating the illegal: On the United Nations and the illegal occupation of Palestine, 1967–2020." European Journal of International Law (2020).ejil.org

Burba, D. "The United Nations and Israeli non-compliance." academia.edu .academia.edu

Leopardi, F. S. "The Popular Front for the Liberation of Palestine during the First Intifada: From opportunity to marginalization (1987–1990)." Political Parties in the Middle East (2020).academia.edu

Gisle, T. "Inverting Goliath An overview of the first Intifada in terms of revolution and ideology." academia.edu .academia.edu

Leopardi, Francesco Saverio, and Francesco Saverio Leopardi. "The First Intifada: Initial Opportunities, Final Marginalisation." The Palestinian Left and Its Decline: Loyal Opposition (2020): 103-140.HTML

Darweish, Marwan. "Popular Resistance in Palestine." Decolonizing the Study of Palestine: Indigenous Perspectives and Settler Colonialism after Elia Zureik (2023): 247.HTML

Naser-Najjab, N. "Palestinian leadership and the contemporary significance of the First Intifada." Race & Class (2020).sagepub.com

Jabali, O. "Popular Resistance against Israeli Territorial Expropriation: Beita as a Model." Middle East Policy (2022).najah.edu

Gandhi, E. L. E. "Archipelago of resettlement: Vietnamese refugee settlers and decolonization across Guam and Israel-Palestine." (2022).oapen.org

Zichi, P. "'We Desire Justice First, Then We Will Work for Peace': Clashes of Feminisms and Transnationalism in Mandatory Palestine." TWAIL Rev. (2021).twailr.com

Abdo, N. A. "The Impact of Palestinian Women in the Diaspora." (2021).HTML

Khalidi, R. "The hundred years' war on Palestine: A history of settler colonialism and resistance, 1917–2017." (2020).HTML

Sexton, Jared. "The Palestinian Cause." Solidarity and the

Palestinian Cause: Indigeneity, Blackness, and the Promise of Universality (2023): 159.HTML

Jaber, L. "The Women's Movement in Palestine: A Journey from the First Intifada and the Oslo Peace Accords to Modern Day Fragmentation and Loss." (2020).uu.nl

Morrison, S. "Whither the State? The Oslo Peace Process and Neoliberal Configurations of Palestine." Social Science Quarterly (2020).wiley.com

Nasasra, M. "The politics of exclusion and localization: The Palestinian minority in Israel and the Oslo Accords." Ethnopolitics (2021).researchgate.net

Enderlin, C. "Shattered Dreams: The Failure of the Peace Process in the Middle East, 1995 to 2002." (2021).HTML

Atallah, M. "The international community's role and impact on the Middle East Peace Process." Canadian Foreign Policy Journal (2021).tandfonline.com

Alsoos, I. "From jihad to resistance: the evolution of Hamas's discourse in the framework of mobilization." Middle Eastern Studies (2021).tandfonline.com

Awad, H. "Understanding Hamas." AlMuntaqa (2021).dohainstitute.org

Tamimi, A. "Hamas: from resistance to governance1." THE FUTURE OF PALESTINE AND ISRAEL .academia.edu

Hamed, Q. "The Constant and the Variable in the Ideology of Hamas (2006-2018)." (2021).theses.fr

Keelan, E. P. and Browne, B. C. "Problematising resilience: development practice and the case of Palestine." Development in Practice (2020).academia.edu

Hallaq, Sameh. "The Palestinian labor market over the last

three decades." Levy Economics Institute, Working Papers Series, November (2020).econstor.eu

Brunner, J. and Amrami, G. P. "Emotionalising the Israeli–Palestinian conflict: on the civil society engagements of Israeli mental health professionals in response to the Palestinian uprisings." Emotions and Society (2021).HTML

Hawari, Y. "Defying Fragmentation and the Significance of Unity: A New Palestinian Uprising." Al-Shabaka: The Palestinian Policy Network (2021).al-shabaka.org

Sahhar, Micaela. "Occupied Narrative and the 2021 Unity Intifada." In Racism, Violence and Harm: Ideology, Media and Resistance, pp. 151-177. Cham: Springer International Publishing, 2023.HTML

Ben-Ami, S. "Prophets Without Honor: The 2000 Camp David Summit and the End of the Two-State Solution." (2022).HTML

Dekel, U. and Moran-Gilad, L. "The Annapolis Process: A Missed Opportunity for a Two-State Solution?." (2021).inss.org.il

Ben-Ami, S. "Prophets Without Honor: The 2000 Camp David Summit and the End of the Two-State Solution." (2022).HTML

Kurtzer, D. C. "The Ingredients of Palestinian-Israeli Peacemaking." Journal of South Asian and Middle Eastern Studies (2020).HTML

Nijim, M. "Genocide in Gaza: Physical destruction and beyond." (2020).umanitoba.ca

Raby, S. "The humanitarian crisis of the Israeli occupation and settler colonialism in the West Bank and Gaza." (2023).emich.edu

Loewenstein, A. "The Palestine Laboratory: How Israel Exports the Technology of Occupation Around the World." (2023).HTML

Lustick, I. S. and Shils, N. "The Palestinians, Israel, and BDS: Strategies and Struggles in Wars of Position." Israel Studies Review (2022).HTML

Baig, M. "Breaking apart the call for boycott, divestment, and sanctions (BDS): dispossession and displacement as two faces of settler colonialism." (2022).mcgill.ca

Alakhras, B. and Ariffin..., R. N. R. "DYNAMICS OF SETTLER COLONIALISM: INFLUENCING FACTORS ON THE ISRAELI TREATMENT TOWARDS THE PALESTINIANS." Al-Shajarah: Journal of the ... (2022).iium.edu.my

Saleh, M. M. "The Palestine Strategic Report 2020-2021." (2022).HTML

De Cesari, C. "Creative institutionalism: Statecraft beyond the state in Palestine." Urban Recovery (2021).researchgate.net

Boren, M. E. "Student Resistance in the Age of Chaos Book 2, 2010-2021: Social Media, Women's Rights, and the Rise of Activism in a Time of Nationalism, Mass ...." (2022).HTML

Slitine, M. "The "Metamorphoses of the Political" in the Contemporary Art of Palestinian Post-Oslo Generation." The Global Politics of Artistic Engagement (2022).HTML

Corm, G. "Arab political thought: past and present." (2020).HTML

Jones, C. "Gaza and the great march of return: Enduring violence and spaces of wounding." Transactions of the Institute of British Geographers (2023).wiley.com

Pace, M., Shehada, M., and Mustafa, Z. A. "Interpolating Gazans' non-violence: Responsibilities in the academy and the media." Partecipazione e conflitto (2021).ruc.dk

Stefanini, P. "Incendiary Kites and Balloons: Anti-Colonial Resistance in Palestine's Great March of Return." Partecipazione e conflitto (2021).unisalento.it

Harrold, David. "From sumud to intifada: Supporting non-violent action to enhance mental health." International Journal of Applied Psychoanalytic Studies 17, no. 2 (2020): 165-182.HTML

El Kurd, D. "Support for violent versus non-violent strategies in the Palestinian territories." Middle East Law and Governance (2022).HTML

Finkelstein, N. "Gaza: An inquest into its martyrdom." (2021).HTML

Schleifer, R. "The 2018-19 Gaza Fence clashes: a case study in psychological warfare." Israel Affairs (2022).HTML

Uddin, H. H. "A HISTORICAL STUDY OF THE INTIFADA MOVEMENTS IN PALESTINE." Pakistan Journal of International Affairs (2022).pjia.com.pk

References For Further Reading

Arambam Noni, and Kangujam Sanatomba. 2015. *Colonialism and Resistance*. Routledge.

Adams, Jefferson. 2014. *Strategic Intelligence in the Cold War and Beyond*. Routledge.

Arambam Noni, and Kangujam Sanatomba. 2015. *Colonialism and Resistance*. Routledge.

Atack, Margaret. 1989. *Literature and the French Resistance : Cultural Politics and Narrative Forms, 1940-1950*. Manchester, Uk ; New York: Manchester University Press ; New York, Ny, Usa.

Awad, Sarah H, Brady Wagoner, and Springerlink (Online Service. 2017. *Street Art of Resistance*. Cham: Springer International Publishing.

Balbi, Gabriele. 2023. *The Digital Revolution*. Oxford University Press.

Best, S. 2014. *The Politics of Total Liberation*. Springer.

Britt, Christopher, Paul Fenn, and Eduardo Subirats. 2018. *Enlightenment in an Age of Destruction : Intellectuals, World Disorder, and the Politics of Empire*. Cham: Palgrave Macmillan.

Carol Dougherty, Leslie Kurke, and Cambridge University Press. *The Cultures Within Ancient Greek Culture: Contact, Conflict, Collaboration*. Cambridge: Cambridge University Press, 2003.

C. David North. 2015. *World War II: The Resistance*. New Word City.

Caygill, Howard. 2013. *On Resistance*. A&C Black.

Coleman, William D. *Property, Territory, Globalization: Struggles over Autonomy*. Vancouver: UBC Press, 2011.

Collins, John J., and Joseph Gilbert Manning. 2016. *Revolt and Resistance in the Ancient Classical World and the near East : In the Crucible of Empire*. Leiden: Brill.

Dann, Otto, and John Rowland Dinwiddy. 1988. *Nationalism in the Age of the French Revolution*. London: Hambledon Press.

D.D., Kosambi. *The Culture and Civilisation of Ancient India in Historical Outline*. S. Chand Publishing, 1994.

Dodd, Gwilym, Helen Lacey, and Anthony Musson. 2021. *People, Power and Identity in the Late Middle Ages*. Routledge.

Duncker, Max. 2023. *The History of the Ancient Civilizations*. DigiCat.

Fagan, Brian, and Chris Scarre. *Ancient Civilizations*. London: Routledge, 2015.

Frère, Bruno, and Marc Jacquemain. 2019. *Everyday Resistance*. Springer Nature.

Garrard, Virginia, Mark Atwood Lawrence, and Julio Moreno. 2013. *Beyond the Eagle's Shadow : New Histories of Latin America's Cold War*. Albuquerque: University Of New Mexico Press.

Gerits, Frank. 2023. *The Ideological Scramble for Africa*. Cornell University Press.

Given, James B. 2019. *Inquisition and Medieval Society Power, Discipline, and Resistance in Languedoc*. Cornell University Press.

Greenstein, Ran. 2022. *Anti-Colonial Resistance in South Africa and Israel/Palestine*. Taylor & Francis.

Gros, Frederic. 2020. *Disobey*. Verso Books.

Harlow, Barbara. 2023. *Resistance Literature*. Taylor & Francis.

Hearsey, John. 2003. *Renaissance and Revolt*. Cambridge University Press.

Hickey-Moody, Anna, and Tara Page. 2015. *Arts, Pedagogy and Cultural Resistance*. Rowman & Littlefield.

Hobsbawm, E J. 2000. *The Age of Revolution : Europe 1789-1848*. London: Phoenix.

Hobsbawm, Eric J. 1962. *The Age of Revolution, 1789-1848*. Signet Book.

Huart, Clement. *Ancient Persia and Iranian Civilization*. London: Routledge, 2013.

J. Keri Cronin, and Kirsty Robertson. 2011. *Imagining Resistance*. Wilfrid Laurier Univ. Press.

John Vignaux Smyth. 1996. *Cross-Addressing : Resistance Literature and Cultural Borders*. Albany (N.Y.): State University Of New York Press, Cop.

K. Bollermann, T Izbicki, and C. Nederman. 2014. *Religion, Power, and Resistance from the Eleventh to the Sixteenth Centuries*. Springer.

Kingston, A.J. 101AD. *D-Day Chronicles*. A.J. Kingston.

Laachir, Karima, and Saeed Talajooy. 2013. *Resistance in Contemporary Middle Eastern Cultures : Literature, Cinema and Music*. New York: Routledge.

Malik, Sarita, Churnjeet Mahn, Michael Pierse, and Ben Rogaly. 2020. *Creativity and Resistance in a Hostile World*. Manchester University Press.

Mcmahon, Darrin M. 2002. *Enemies of the Enlightenment : The French Counter-Enlightenment and the Making of Modernity*. Oxford ; New York: Oxford University Press.

Miller, Daniel, Michael Rowlands, and Chris Tilley. 2005. *Domination and Resistance*. Routledge.

Moffat, Alexander, Alan Riach, and Linda Macdonald-Lewis. 2020. *Arts of Resistance*. Luath Press Ltd.

Mooney, Catherine M. 2016. *Clare of Assisi and the Thirteenth-Century Church : Religious Women, Rules, and Resistance*. Philadelphia: University Of Pennsylvania Press.

Moussa Traoré, and Tony Talburt. 2017. *Fight for Freedom : Black Resistance and Identity*. Legon-Accra, Ghana Sub-Saharan Publishers.

Pnina Werbner, and Richard Werbner. 2002. *Postcolonial Subjectivities in Africa*. Zed Books.

Raisa Maria Toivo, and Sari Katajala-Peltomaa. 2016. *Lived Religion and the Long Reformation in Northern Europe C. 1300–1700*. BRILL.

Raschke, Carl A. 2003. *The Digital Revolution and the Coming of the Postmodern University*. London: Routledgefalmer.

Raymond William Baker. 2015. *One Islam, Many Worlds of Muslims : Spirituality, Identity, and Resistance across Islamic Lands*. New York: Oxford University Press.

Sahle, Eunice N. 2018. *Human Rights in Africa : Contemporary Debates and Struggles*. New York: Palgrave Macmillan.

Salmi, Hannu. *19th Century Europe: A Cultural History*. Hoboken: John Wiley & Sons, 2013.

Salmi, Hannu. 2013. *19th Century Europe*. John Wiley & Sons.

Simon Shui-Man Kwan. 2013. *Postcolonial Resistance and Asian Theology*. Routledge.

Sorba, Carlotta, and Enrico Francia. 2021. *Political Objects in the Age of Revolution : Material Culture, National Identities, Political Practices*. Roma: Viella.

Viet Thanh Nguyen. 2002. *Race & Resistance : Literature & Politics in Asian America*. New York: Oxford University Press.

Wyrtzen, Jonathan. 2016. *Making Morocco Colonial Intervention and the Politics of Identity*. Cornell University Press.

Zysman, John, and Abraham Newman. 2006. *How Revolutionary Was the Digital Revolution? : National Responses, Market Transitions, and Global Technology*. Palo Alto, Calif.: Stanford University Press.

www.ingramcontent.com/pod-product-compliance
Lightning Source LLC
Chambersburg PA
CBHW071458080526
44587CB00014B/2139